I Laughed First

Alicia Cardway

Published by AJ CARDWAY BOOKS, 2022.

I LAUGHED FIRST

First edition. November 16, 2022.

Written by Alicia Cardway.

Table of Contents

INTRODUCTION 1
PART I - TURKEY 7
THE ASSIGNMENT 8
THE ARRIVAL 10
THE SISTERS—PART I 12
THE PEOPLE 16
THE DISCOTHEQUE 19
THE ROYALS 20
THE PORCELAIN HOLE 23
THE MOSH PIT 25
THE BIRTH 30
THE PRESCHOOL 35
THE CHARADES—PART I 38
THE RIVER 41
THE FULL NELSON 43
THE HOLIDAYS 48
THE MARKET 52
THE SISTERS—PART II 54
THE CHARADES—PART II 56
THE BANK 59
THE GYM 61
THE SISTERS—PART III 63
THE ROYALS—PART II 66
THE SISTERS—PART IV 68
THE HAMMAM 70
THE HAMMAM—THROUGH MIA'S EYES 75
THE FALL 79
THE ROYALS—PART III 84
THE STARING 86
THE LOVELY EMPLOYMENT 88
THE LIST 90

THE DEPARTURE—TURKEY 93
PART II - BELGIUM 94
THE MEANTIME 95
THE FIRST WEEK 96
THE JOB 99
THE UNJOB 102
THE DEATH TRAP 103
THE BISE 105
THE HARD THINGS 106
THE FRENCHEMIES 109
THE WORLD IS YOUR PLAYGROUND URINAL 112
THE FAKE FRIENDS 115
THE LUXEMBOURG CEMETERY 117
THE CONFRONTATION 120
THE NERVOUS MOTHER—PART I 123
THE NEW FRIENDS 125
THE BISE—PART II 129
THE FRENCH BLUNDERS BEGIN—PART I 131
THE FALL—ROUND II 133
THE HALLOWEEN PARTIES 136
THE FRENCH CLASS 139
THE NERVOUS MOTHER—PART II 144
THE REAL JOB—PART I 147
THE COMPLIMENT 149
THE REAL JOB—PART II 151
THE BREATHALYZER 152
THE BREAKFAST CLUB 154
THE REAL JOB—PART III 157
THE FRENCH BLUNDERS—PART II 158
THE PLAYDATE—PART I 161
THE FRENCH BLUNDERS—PART III 162
THE FRENCH BLUNDERS—PART IV 164
THE JOKE 166

THE UNDERWEAR 171

THE SMELL 173

THE LUXEMBOURG CEMETERY—PART II 175

THE PLAYDATE—PART II 179

THE FRENCH BLUNDERS—PART V 184

THE FRENGLISH 186

THE MOM FAIL 188

THE FRENCH BLUNDERS—PART VI 190

THE VIOLENT AMERICANS 192

THE OLD MEN 195

THE ORDERLY 197

THE STEREOTYPE 201

THE MAMMOGRAM 205

THE DEPARTURE—BELGIUM 209

THE MEANTIME—PART II 211

To my Littles and my Love – you have my whole heart.

PROLOGUE

It's been six months since we moved to Belgium, and I figured it's time to put on my big girl panties and really try to learn *le francais*. This language has already beaten me up and stomped on me and if this is going to be a fair fight, I need to train the right way.

At the suggestion (forceful insistence) of a woman in our neighborhood, I looked up the local adult language school and decided to get more information. I hesitantly arrived at the address and after a few wrong attempts, I found the school – which happened to be a convent.

Mumbling to myself under my breath (I have to give myself pep talks or I'll go insane – which ironically is what makes me look insane to any passerby), I knocked on the door and was greeted by the Sisters.

After a flurry of words machine-gunned in my direction and before I even knew what was happening, I was following a nun down a long hallway and led into a room where I was being introduced to seven other adults sitting there.

"Uhhh, *Bonjour,*" I said.

"*Bonjour et bienvenue,*" they replied in unison.

I started to turn around and leave, but I ran straight into the nun who was *not* leaving. In fact, she turned me right back around by the shoulders and I felt a little nudge on my back. She was literally pushing me (kindly) to sit down.

"Oh no, dear. You can sit right there. This is your class," is what I assumed she was saying, although I wasn't sure. It could have been "Fat chance, American. You will learn French and you will LIKE it." *Oh? Oh...We're doing this* now. *OK, this is happening. It's happening right now.* I could feel the heat rising up my neck and *this,* my friends, is the point when I start to become a little silly. You see, living overseas is a sure way for self-discovery and I have discovered that I turn into somewhat of a flighty clown when I'm extremely uncomfortable. I make funny jokes in order to divert the tears.

"Bonjour à tous! Je suis une femme! (Hello all! I am a woman!)" I announced, trying to break the ice. They laughed and I cried a little inside. Then the class continued...excepttttt I realized that everyone in the class speaks French already. I raised my hand, hesitantly, barely two inches above the table to ask if I was in the right place.

"Um...*c'est la classe pour les débutants*?" (It is the class for beginners?)

"Oui! Oui!"

"Okkkk, *mais tout parler français*? (Okkkk, but all to speak French?)." What I was trying to ask was, "Why does everyone already speak French?" She understood me though because she responded S-L-O-W-L-Y, miming the actions with her lips as much as with her hands, "They. are. here. to. learn. how. to. read. and. write. French!"

Was it that obvious I didn't really speak French? So now I'm attending a language school to try and learn French with adult native French speakers.

Touché, French. Touché.

INTRODUCTION

I was seven years old when one day I found myself staring at my dad's business shirts hanging in his closet. I could see the bottom of the red spear from behind the shirts leaning against the wall, taunting me. "*Go on, little girl, pick me up. See what happens.*" My still-developing brain debated between curiosity and what I thought was surely impending doom and punishment from The Red Spear gods. I stood there a moment longer and then parted the business shirts in the same way I imagined Moses had parted the Red Sea. (Clearly, the drama and theatrics started young for me). There it was in its full woman-forbidding glory. It was made from wood and painted red with other accenting colors. The entire length was about four and a half feet tall with the top six inches forming a point, separating it from the rest of the spear with a ring of tribal ribbon and dangling feathers. It had two inset stones that looked like giant, angry eyes. The spear was intimidating and although I was hesitant, I had to find out what would happen if I touched it.

I had been so annoyed when my dad explained to me that girls were not allowed to touch this "sacred" spear. It was a Maori tribal chief's spear from New Zealand that my dad had received when he lived there years before I was born. He had brought the spear out one evening and explained that the *Rakau Taiaha* was only for male warriors and in ancient times, women were not allowed to touch it. We needed to respect the tradition or it would bring dishonor. All I heard was "Blah blah blah."

He took the spear back upstairs, hid it, and I forgot about it until I was in my parents' closet that day and saw the bottom of the staff sticking out from below my dad's shirts. I reached my shaking pointer finger out and barely skimmed it. *Huh, nothing happened. No lightning or earthquakes. Well, maybe just a little more then.* Still nothing. So obviously I did what any curious seven-year-old would do and I grabbed it and practically just licked it from top to bottom to really tempt the Red Spear gods. Pretty soon I was tribal-warrior training around the walk-in closet with the spear pretending to fight the men that had decided women shouldn't touch it. Meanies!

That entire experience is the earliest memory I have of learning about another culture. It was like the spear had popped a metaphorical bubble around me and I started to see a little clearer and realize that there was something else that existed outside my little realm of familiarity. And by that, I mean the predominantly Caucasian, Middle-class, Midwestern suburbs. The Maori tribal spear experience had sparked a new and budding awareness and I was ready to see the world! Unfortunately, I don't think it wanted to see me.

Riding the wave of a childhood curiosity to learn more about other cultures, I saved and scrimped for an internship in Mexico during my undergraduate studies where I could visit orphanages and study Spanish. This, my friends, is where the fun begins. I (naively) imagined becoming bilingual in a few weeks' time and assimilating so easily into the culture that you would never have known I was really American underneath. My flighty ignorance wasn't prepared for how difficult, or funny, it would be to live in a completely different environment and language. Not only did I not expect such little cultural differences to have such a big impact, but I had no idea that my four years of high school Spanish was more Gringo-Spanish than ACTUAL Spanish.

One day my host *Mama* told me that someone called for me while I was out. When I asked, in Spanish, who it was, she said, "Louder." So I said louder, "Who was it?" and when she said, "Louder," again,

I yelled, "WHO WAS IT?!!" (I thought maybe she had a hearing problem). Finally, she just handed me the paper with the name "Laura" on it. Her Spanish accent and rolling the "R" made the name Laura sound like "louder" in English. I immediately started laughing and tried to explain to the family and the other foreign students staying there what happened. No one laughed—maybe out of fear of being rude? Maybe because they couldn't decipher anything with my thick American accent? I don't know, but I looked around, almost begging someone to laugh with me..no one was. So I did what I've always done – I wrote about it.

As a child, I kept a journal with the intention to help Future-Me remember everything. As a teenager, I kept a journal to help then Present-Me survive adolescence, and as a young adult, I kept a journal to help Future-Mini-Mes know their mother. Now, as a full-fledged adult, I keep a journal because it's cheaper than therapy.

Telling and writing my stories down has been a release for me because so many of my stories have been so embarrassing or awkward. It has made them less humiliating if I a) laugh about them first, b) laugh *with* someone else, and c) embrace self-deprecation in a safe, healthy way.

These habits started at a young age, actually. I come from a large family—seven children—and you better believe that if one of us made a mistake of any kind, it was immediately noticed and joked about. Publicly. Not maliciously, of course, but in an "it's my sibling duty to laugh at you" kind of way. My family is loud and fun and full of laughter—most of which results from something funny one of us has done or said. Think big, Italian, Catholic family, but... neither Italian nor Catholic. I, being the oldest child, was admittedly one of the first to point out someone's mistake and laugh until my siblings became old enough to realize and point out MY mishaps. It backfired pretty quickly. So I developed a defense mechanism: If I made a blunder or did something embarrassing, I immediately pointed it out and made sure I was the FIRST one to laugh about it. Voila. Self-deprecation as dignity preservation.

After Mexico, I returned to the States, graduated from university, and started dating Aaron. He is truly a kind, intelligent, and downright gorgeous specimen who had previously lived in Greece for two years and was as keen as I was to see more of the world. We didn't know when, where or how it would happen, but we had big plans. We were married the following year and five years after that, we had our first child, a boy named Will. By that time, we were living in the Northern Virginia area, near Washington, D.C., and looking for opportunities to go abroad. Finally, when Will turned two, we got our first opportunity with a job in Turkey.

As our life overseas was just beginning, I was flooded with so many new situations—faster than I could write. I hadn't been ready for the culture shock or the language barriers to be so extreme and I wished so badly that someone was there to laugh, gasp—and cry— with me, so I continued journaling and started sharing some of the stories with family and friends back home in the States. With each country and culture came new and distinct stories to tell.

These stories took on a whole new meaning when our children grew and started to have similar experiences and in order to encourage them to find humor in the face of hard things or embarrassment, I shared with them some of my own personal experiences. While preparing dinner one night, I listened to my children's giggles as they read aloud some of my writings from living overseas. As they continued reading stories, their giggles turned into full-blown belly laughter. "Mom," my son said chuckling, "this is just like *Diary of A Wimpy Kid*...except for moms!" I chose to take that as a compliment since he's read the series three times.

"Are you calling me a wimpy mom?" I retorted, then stopped, thinking out loud, "*Diary of a Wimpy Mom* would be a great title for my current journal." That's the first time I thought about compiling all these stories in a book to give to my children for Christmas. Like many mothers, there is an abundance of principles I want to teach my children, but one principal near the top of that list is resilience—and recognizing that I'm more of a storyteller than a prolific writer—the best way I know how to teach resilience is through laughter.

Years ago I read an article titled, *If We Can Laugh at It, We Can Live with It.* The author, Brad Wilcox, says:

> With a humorous viewpoint and a shared laugh, an uncomfortable situation [can] become bearable. Humor helps. Humor heals....Humor allows us to view our lives in a more positive light, deal with personal conflicts and intolerance, and cope with trials and frustrations that might otherwise seem overwhelming.

We all experience some sort of discomfort—that's what life is, right? It's full of circumstances that we can't control but full of responses that we can. (Although I realize we *chose* to go overseas, I didn't choose to have my pride slaughtered and handed to me on a silver platter). Obviously, not every situation is meant to be a laughing matter, but we can find humor in so many scenarios. I just happen to find humor in uncomfortable foreign situations. Or, more accurately, uncomfortable foreign situations find humor in me.

For anyone who has ever found themself laughing in uncomfortable awkward situations, this book is for you. For anyone who needs to learn to laugh in awkward situations, this book is also for you. It is a compilation of my journal entries, letters to family, and social media posts that focus on the two countries in which we have spent the majority of our time: Turkey, where the cultural differences blindsided me, and Belgium where the language barrier put me in a three-year chokehold. Every one of these experiences opened my eyes and made the world seem bigger (or, more accurately, me seem smaller) and instilled love and respect for cultural diversity and for doing hard things. While these stories are only parts of my journals, with some added details for context, they are real and they are raw.

They are me and I laughed first.

All names have been changed to protect anonymity and privacy.

PART I - TURKEY

There are no foreign lands.
It is the traveler only who is foreign.
-Robert Louis Stevenson

THE ASSIGNMENT

Stateside, December, six months before Turkey

The stars have aligned and we found a job overseas – in Turkey! We leave this summer and it just so happens that we recently found out we are pregnant with Baby Number Two. I will be about seven or eight months pregnant when we move and I'm not sure yet if I'll stay and have the baby here or go and have the baby in Turkey. Either way, this will be an adventure. I have an adventurous spirit and I'm comfortable with change, which I credit to moving more than six times and attending seven different schools all before the age of fourteen. I've done it before and I can do it again. Right?

When Aaron and I were dating years ago, he thought about breaking up with me. *Thought* being the key word. He was worried that if we really did get married and moved overseas, that I wouldn't be able to handle all the change and living away from my family. Some nonsense about, "Just because you like to Salsa dance and speak a little Spanish doesn't mean you're ready to leave everything you're comfortable with." Well, joke's on him.

So now Aaron is in language classes for the next few months in preparation for our move and I just signed up for a community class to learn some basic Turkish. I have no idea what to expect. The only knowledge I have of Turkey is from the movie *Taken* with Liam Neeson and any time I mention to someone that we're moving there, without fail, the movie *Midnight Express* is mentioned. You know, the one with all the torture scenes in a Turkish prison. Yeah, so comforting, but any other expat family I've ever met that has lived there said they fell in love with it and would give anything to go back.

I remember daydreaming during class one day in high school and trying to imagine where I would be in ten years and I promise you this—never in my wildest dreams did the possibility of delivering a baby and living in Turkey come to mind. It's funny where life takes us.

THE ARRIVAL

T*urkey, July, month one*
    Note to self: Bring ski masks the next time you decide to waste all your points and spare change moving up to business class on a transatlantic flight. Why? Because our flight, unfortunately, was very eventful and ski masks would have hidden our identity (and shame) so no one would know who ruined their premium seats on a RED-EYE FLIGHT with a screaming two year old. Apparently, we sleep-trained our son *too* well because he won't sleep anywhere but his bed. Knowing that this flight was red-eye and Will would need a bed to sleep in, we used ALL our points to bump up to business class so we could have the chairs that turned into beds. Our. Poor. Fellow. Passengers. Will screamed for a good four hours. He would not go to sleep and I couldn't walk around the airplane with him because of my giant, offending pregnant belly, so Aaron literally walked the aisles the entire night trying to get Will to go to sleep. All the lights were out and I'm pretty sure every earplug on that plane was used. I had so much anxiety because I knew other people paid good money to be able to sleep all night in that section. Nope. No one slept. I have no idea if I was receiving pity looks or sneers because I couldn't even look anyone in the eyes as we disembarked. If you're wondering, Will never fell asleep, but we are finally here.

    As we drove through the city and streets to our new home, I was having trouble processing my feelings and thoughts. It was foreign, but beautiful, but dirty, all at the same time. We turned onto our street and the sidewalks were crumbling and weeds were everywhere. There was an abandoned building next to a brand new bank and then a crumbling market and then our beautiful new building surrounded by a cement wall. I think I expected certain areas of the city to be prosperous and certain areas to be run down, but I didn't expect it to change from one building to the next. Here you have extravagance and poverty right next to each other.

As we pulled up in front of our building, Will decided THIS was the time to fall asleep. He had been awake for over twenty-four hours and his little body couldn't take it anymore. We carried him inside our new home, found the beds, and all of us immediately fell asleep.

THE SISTERS—PART I

T*urkey, July, month one*
    I have never felt so out of place IN MY LIFE. What in the WORLD was I thinking when I claimed to be "an adventurous spirit" and "comfortable with change"? Stupid, stupid girl. I'm a simple girl that grew up in the 'burbs. I've always been a confident person (admittedly sometimes too confident), but if you want a piece of reality and humble pie, move overseas. Want a big slice? Choose a place where the culture, language, and religion are all distinctly different. Want a bigger slice? Move there eight months pregnant.

Less than twenty-four hours after we landed and still in a jet-lag induced state, Aaron informed me he was leaving for work. I panicked. We had no food. No TV. No internet. And no phone. What we DID have was a two-year-old.

"What about milk for Will?!" I panicked.

"Just walk to a market and buy some. My colleague left some cash for us until we can get some Lira," said the husband who has already lived two-and-a-half years in neighboring Greece. This is child's play to him. He left and I double bolted the door and stared through the peephole for a good ten minutes. I actually don't know what I expected to see, but I felt trapped in a box (although it is a gorgeous apartment). I felt like a lab rat inspecting its new digs—sniffing and touching everything and every little corner; trying all the buttons and knobs and opening everything. After sufficiently inspecting the entire apartment, including the new-to-me bidet toilet, I said a quick prayer and a Hail Mary (anything helps at this point) and ventured out in search of food for our child. I felt like a pioneer woman. I felt proud, buuuut that lasted for all of a millisecond.

I knew the words "Hello" and "How are you?" in Turkish, but that wouldn't get me anywhere buying milk. I somehow made it to the market and found a jar with a cow on it, praying it was milk, and ran (waddled) back and double bolted the door again.

The first week was a blur. We slowly became acquainted with the city and transportation systems. We walked the neighborhoods and local parks. I soon noticed, very self-consciously, that I was getting looks of disdain everywhere we went. Was it because I am noticeably American and historically the Turks and Americans have been on rocky terms? Aaron blends right in with any Middle Eastern or Levant country (dumb chameleon), but even with my darker hair, I have a hard time. I noticed lips curling up and clucks of the tongue when walking past women and realized they were looking at my belly! I felt naked all of a sudden. What was wrong?! It dawned on me that I hadn't seen a single pregnant woman since we'd been there. There were two women in particular that I could see talking about me and when I told Aaron how uncomfortable I felt with them looking at me and my belly, he leaned down and practically made out with my belly! I felt really naked then. He winked at them and I'm telling you, I'm shocked they didn't have a heart attack. It probably doesn't help that I have been wearing skin-tight shirts—and not the kind I used to be in trouble for wearing in high school—the maternity kind that stretches so far it starts to ripple because my belly is so big. The kind that does nothing to hide my protruding belly button. Later on, I discovered that it's considered "immodest" and "offensive" to many Turks for pregnant women to be so "exposed." In fact, unbeknownst to me, there were protests in Istanbul for this very thing. People gathered in the streets to protest against shaming pregnant women for being in public.

On the way back from one of our exploratory walks, we had the opportunity to finally meet our neighbors directly across the hall.

English speakers would refer to them as Spinster Sisters, but that has somewhat of a negative connotation. However, when you read "Spinster Sisters" an image popped into your head, didn't it? Well, that's exactly what they look like so go with it. They are single, never been married, sisters with matching, slightly varying names, in their late fifties, early sixties. Belgin and Bilge. Well-dressed, but not necessarily well-kempt. Wealthy, but apparently not enough to want to put a bra on. They were talkative and polite, but not warm and friendly. This was the hardest personality for me to read when I base so much of my understanding of Turkish conversations on facial expressions.

Aaron, the ever-friendly person that he is, immediately introduced our family, speaking Turkish. He was charming, handsome, and charismatic and I was just nodding profusely and raising my eyebrows as if they—my eyebrows—could speak Turkish and participate in the conversation. All of a sudden the conversation stopped and they looked at me quietly. Immediately aware of the unwanted attention, I started ~~peein~~ sweating and asked my husband through smiling teeth, ventriloquist style, "What? What are they looking at? Why are they looking at me?" He started to look a little nervous and shrugged his shoulders, but more at them as if he was answering their question, not mine.

Belgin disappeared and we stood there awkwardly until she came back a few seconds later carrying something. It wasn't until she bent over and placed it on the floor that I realized IT. WAS. A. SCALE. I let out a *lasp* (that's a laugh and a gasp in case you're wondering—I make strange noises in awkward situations for which there are no words) and pleaded with Aaron (still ventriloquist style) to rescue me from the situation. The sisters kept speaking rapidly in Turkish, which still just sounds like a bunch of oo's and zz's to me, and pointed at me to get on the scale. I—who had spent the last eight months telling the nurses at all my appointments that I didn't want to know my weight each and every time, because "It's not about the weight, it's about the baby" (and the 7-Eleven taquitos; don't judge)—was being told in Turkish to step on the scale so they could...gawk? admire? chastise?... my weight. So guess what I did? I stepped on.

They immediately peered at the numbers and started speaking to each other in rapid, excited Turkish, but because their faces didn't seem to move, I couldn't discern their general thought about what the numbers revealed. I kept asking Aaron, "What?! What are they saying? Translate!" but he denied being able to understand them. (He's a liar and the best husband in the world.) Their heads bobbed back and forth and they let out a few *hmmm*'s and then just as abruptly, they picked up the scale, said their pleasantries, and bid us farewell. Even after Aaron took Will into our apartment I still just stood there trying to comprehend what had just happened. I stood there long enough for the light sensors to turn off. I still have no idea what they said or why they wanted to weigh me.

Welcome to Turkey.

THE PEOPLE

T urkey, July, month one
    In addition to our weight-obsessed neighbors, we've been able to get out and meet our street neighbors. The street we live on is like a family in a way because everyone lives in apartments and so close together and they are constantly walking to the markets or going to the restaurants so we see each other all the time. We've been able to get to know everyone better in the weeks we've been here, and we've been informally inducted into the neighborhood family.

    Our building manager is named Kerem and he rings our doorbell twice a day to say, "Market?" just in case I need anything. I wouldn't know how to tell him if I did. He often sees me coming back to the house with a screaming and kicking toddler and will run out to get the door, saying the same thing to me every time, "*Çok sıcak*" (pronounced Choke See-jock) which means, "Very hot." I'm not sure if he means the weather or if he thinks it's hot that a pregnant foreign lady is wrestling a tantrum-throwing toddler.

    The other night Kerem came to the door to collect trash. Normally he's in jeans and a T-shirt, but this time he was in a suit. Being the (sometimes) overly friendly person that I am, I wanted to tell him he looked so nice and so I said, "Oh! *Çok güzel!*!" And he just laughed and said, "*Teşekkürler,*" and left blushing. Aaron then told me I basically told him he was "So pretty! So yummy!" Apparently, you usually say *Çok güzel* when something is beautiful or when referring to really good food. Bless my heart—I'm trying here.

Directly across from our building is a fancy restaurant with a valet service managed by Mustafa Bey, the same one who has endless pockets of candy for Will. Mustafa is my height (maybe shorter), in his sixties with missing teeth, and walks with a limp due to a "bum leg." I've seriously contemplated kidnapping him when we leave here so I could just take him home with us.

Past a few apartment buildings and small pizza places, there is the coolest restaurant at the end of our street. It is straight out of a Greek island with plants hanging everywhere and little lights in the trees overhead. The whole floor is made up of broken sea glass and pottery pasted in cement. The owner is a forty-year-old woman who just holds my hand every time I see her and talks to me like I know Turkish. The first time we met, she made me sit down and placed before me something that was supposed to be eaten and honestly, I was scared for my unborn baby's life. It literally looked like raw salmon with green jelly and then a cup of mayonnaise with nuts on top. Not wanting to be rude, I hesitantly tasted it and it was...heavenly. My taste buds have never experienced those flavors together. After some translation, we discovered it was eggplant jelly with pudding on top. It still sounds disgusting, but I swear my taste buds partied that night.

Just across the intersection is the market we frequent—the same one I ran to for milk on the first day. We've since been able to meet the owner and the staff, and I look forward to our daily interactions. I normally buy fresh vegetables and fruits as well as eggs and milk; however, I stopped buying the eggs for a while because of the "coloring" of the yolks. At first, I thought I bought a bad batch because their egg yolks were orange...not yellow. I threw that carton away and later bought another carton. Their yolks were orange too. Like pumpkin-orange. I attributed the egg color to being rotten from the lack of refrigeration because they just have the cartons on a regular aisle. I spoke to a friend one day and told her about the strange orange-yolk eggs here. She laughed and told me that means they really are farm fresh and grass-fed. Something about higher Omega-3s. Well, don't I just feel stupid for throwing away perfectly good eggs.

Next to the market, at the intersection, is a *simit* stand. *Simit* (pronounced See-meet) are like Turkish bagels and that's what everyone has for breakfast. A *Simitçi* is a man who sells *Simits*. *Simitçis* will walk around the neighborhoods and streets with a huge platter (like three feet in diameter) with a hundred *Simits* on their head yelling, "*Simitçi*!!!!!" Then people will yell down to him from their apartment windows and he stops and waits for the person to come and buy the *Simits*. Will thinks the man that walks around every morning in our neighborhood yelling is really named *Simit*. So Will walks around the house with plates on his head yelling, "Suh-meeeeeee-cheese" like the man does. When Will sees him outside he'll go running and yell, "Hi, Simit!" They are fifty cents and pretty yummy and you don't even have to go find them...they find *you*. It's like one step up from a drive-thru. So convenient. Take notes, people, take notes.

THE DISCOTHEQUE

T*urkey, July, month one*
     I experienced my first discotheque in Turkey. It's probably not what you would expect to hear from an almost eight-months-pregnant woman, but nonetheless, I did.

I'm getting used to my apartment and all the little odd (to me) differences from my usual living arrangements. For example, I desperately miss ice makers and air conditioners. One of the other quirks about this apartment, and maybe all the others as well, is that the light switches are on the outside of the rooms and they flip the opposite way. To turn the light on, you flip the switch down. Now that just doesn't make sense, does it? It also doesn't seem right to be taking a shower and you've locked the door and your two-year-old decides to play with the light switches OUTSIDE the bathroom...so you get a discotheque-style light show while showering. On the verge of seizing, you yell at him to leave the lights alone and after another full minute of hallucination-induced light flickering, he walks away and leaves you in the dark because he thinks he's kept the light on by turning the switch UP when it's actually DOWN to keep the lights on.

I saw this shower going differently in my head.

THE ROYALS

T*urkey, August, month two*
One of the biggest cultural differences I noticed in the first two weeks of being here is how the Turks treat children. When I say that it's like walking down the street with a celebrity—that is the understatement of the century. Children are revered and treated like a deity. No one had prepared me for this, except to say, "Turks love kids." Um, there needs to be an *entire* book written just on this cultural phenomenon alone. As hard as it is to move to a new country with a two-year-old, mark my words, Will is going to be my saving grace here.

I'm pretty sure I would have become a hermit and never left my safe space if it wasn't for Will or the fact that it is so hot here. It's like being in the Southwestern United States. Hot and dry. That coupled with the lack of air conditioning (because according to the Turks, AC can give you diseases and make you sick), I was in my own personal pregnant hell. When the temperature reached 104 degrees and Will became lethargic, I caved and we left the sauna-like apartment for some fresh air.

We pushed the buttons to the comically small elevator and waited before stepping into the three-by-three-foot space. I can barely fit in there, let alone anyone else. Elevator designers here must have the opposite of claustrophobia...whatever that is called.

Trying to be as inconspicuous as possible to avoid interaction with...well, anyone, we didn't make it ten feet without being stopped by Mustafa Bey, the sweet restaurant valet man on our street. He pulled out a candy from his pocket and gave it to Will and kissed him on top of the head. I graciously smiled and nodded my head, not daring to open my mouth and try to speak Turkish. We'd walked another ten feet when two women stopped and ogled over Will and pulled out two more candies from their purses to give to Will. I figured that maybe every Turk carries around candy with them just in case they might run into a child. Will, on the other hand, started saying "Trick or Treat" to every adult we passed. It's like Halloween every day of the year here.

We made it to the park and I sat my pregnant-self down on the bench and put my head down to avoid any eye contact that might elicit an awkward conversation. Will was climbing all over the playground when I saw a group of guys walking arm-in-arm our way. (Males are affectionate with each other here in a way that is culturally abnormal in the US unless you have same-gender attraction). They were probably in their late teens or early twenties and dressed in tight silk shirts and skinny jeans. The smell of cologne mixed with the lack of deodorant attacked my pregnant nose as this group passed me going towards the little playground. I was amazed that their gelled hair didn't melt in this heat as it was spiked straight up. The next thing I knew, and to my horror, this group of guys grabbed Will and started throwing him in the air. I had no idea what they were saying and I started to panic and frantically look around for help. Will, who is all boy and idolizes older males, was loving the attention and gut laughing. I moved closer to them, not sure what I would do or how fast I could run with an extra fifty pounds on me, but my heart was beating through my chest and my anxiety was through the roof. Without so much as a glance my way, they passed him around and kissed his cheeks and forehead, and set him back down. As quickly as they had come, they had gone. The only thing I could do was stand there staring and thinking, *WHAT IN THE WORLD JUST HAPPENED?!* I felt like I was on a hidden camera show.

The heat was unbearable and I had to pee. Yes, we had only been there fifteen minutes, but I'm on a thirty-minute schedule with this bladder right now. Will immediately started crying when I told him that we needed to go, and I eventually had to pick up a screaming and kicking toddler to carry back home. Walking. In 104-degree weather. Eight months pregnant. Go ahead and take that in for a second. Will was writhing and flailing and hitting me when I noticed this policeman shaking his finger at me from across the street. I glanced behind me to see if he was looking at someone else, but there was no one else. I made my way across the street in his direction and as soon as I got close, he ran over to me and grabbed Will from my arms. *Why do people keep grabbing him?!* He said something to me in Turkish and with tears in my eyes at that point, I just said, "I'm sorry. I don't speak Turkish!" I tried to take Will back, but to my surprise, he got a huge smile on his face and waved my hands away. He gestured a big pregnant belly and then wagged his finger to say "no" and mimed carrying Will. Will was still crying, but less so now that a stranger was holding him (go figure). I mimed pointing to Will and then made the walking motion with my fingers while wagging my other finger "no" hoping that my amazing gift for charades said, "My son is two and is throwing a fit because he wants to stay at the park and he won't walk home by himself and it's hot and I need to get home." The policeman, who I then realized was a security guard at the bank, motioned for me to walk and adjusted Will on his hip so he could carry him better.

Want to know a word that's missing from the English language? It's a word that conveys the feeling of "incredibly awkward" and "extreme and overwhelming gratitude" at the same time. Whatever that word is, I felt it while watching this security guard carrying my crying, writhing toddler alongside me in silence because we are just two people from two different countries and cultures that can't speak the same language, but can understand and appreciate serving your fellow man. Or pregnant woman.

THE PORCELAIN HOLE

T*urkey, August, month two*
    Today I found out I had muscles in parts of my body I didn't even know existed. Sounds fun, right? I've been venturing out a little more, mostly because I made an expat friend who happens to speak Turkish. So pretty much, she's my security blanket. We don't ever venture too far because of my bladder issues, but today we pushed the limits and went a little farther. Can I just say that I am so over being pregnant and needing to use the restroom all the time? Today we went to a bazaar of sorts and of course, I needed to empty my bladder five minutes after getting there. A bazaar is not like a store. It's out in the open or in a big, empty makeshift building. My friend pleaded my case and asked every shop owner if there was a restroom nearby. Finally, we found someone who knew of one down a dark hallway in the basement of a practically deserted building. Curse my pregnant bladder. Promising my friend that I would be fine going alone, I ventured down to the basement. Looking around for the restroom, I finally saw a curtain and pulled it back to reveal "the restroom." I'm not lying when I say a dungeon prison toilet would have been better than that. For a split second, I weighed my options and gave serious consideration to wetting my pants instead.

The "toilet" was a porcelain hole in the ground with about six inches of porcelain on either side of the hole to plant your feet when squatting. The room itself was no more than a forty-eight-inch square. Standing there for a minute trying to formulate a plan of action, I decided to just go for it. I accidentally lost my balance and reached out to steady myself, barely missing the curtain, and inadvertently touched the wall, which was covered in what I sincerely hoped were rust stains. I dry heaved and prayed I wouldn't vomit. Gaining my balance, I tried again. Trying to aim over a hole in the ground as a pregnant woman should be on a Korean game show because it's impossible.

I needed to wash my shoes when I got home.

Typical porcelain toilet found in Turkey (photo by SuSanA Secretariat, Flickr)

THE MOSH PIT

T*urkey, August, month two*
      Part of the allure of working overseas is that we get both US and the host country's holidays off work. Before coming, we planned that we would take advantage of every single holiday and travel as much as we could. Our first holiday came about three weeks after our arrival. We decided to head north with our friend Julie to Safranbolu and Amasra on the Black Sea. Julie borrowed her friend's car because we both just arrived and neither of us have our cars yet. We don't have GPS, and I naively thought printed directions would be sufficient. Oh, the naivety. They probably would have been if the streets had signs. Or asphalt. Once we got on the edge of the city and still had two hours to our destination, we might as well have been trying to navigate using the sun for direction.

      Fortunately, Aaron speaks enough Turkish that we could stop every hundred feet and ask someone. Unfortunately, we've since learned that Turks so desperately want to be helpful that rather than admitting they don't know, they make up directions. I'm not kidding. We were now about two hours into our drive and still about two hours away. Google Maps said the total drive was supposed to be two hours and fifteen minutes. Thank you.

      We finally found a "highway" heading north and quickly realized that rules apparently don't apply when driving here. Our two-lane highway had somehow become five lanes (going fifteen miles per hour). The markings painted on the road must have been for decoration, because where one car should have been (in the right lane), there were three. Side by side, side mirror to side mirror. I could tell what the driver next to us had for breakfast because I was so close I could see the remnants in his teeth. Apparently everyone—including the nine people stuffed into a two-door, five-passenger car next to us, one of which was a sleeping baby on the dashboard—decided to use this *Bayram* (holiday) to head north. We didn't get that memo.

The car we borrowed was akin to an SUV—but without shocks. This would be like riding a roller coaster, except at eight months pregnant, I felt like we were horseback riding the whole way there. Or like I was trapped in a realm of teeter-totters and I was the one that kept slamming onto the concrete.

Normally the urge to empty my bladder comes every thirty minutes, but the lack of shocks shortened that feeling to every three minutes and by this point, I was in pain. Baby girl had decided to use my painfully full bladder as her new squishy pillow. There was literally nothing for miles. In every direction. Just dried dirt and sagebrush and sky. I saw people stopped on the side of the road eating lunch and saying midday prayers. Aaron rolled down his window and asked the guy next to us if there is a city or gas station nearby.

"Not for miles," he said.

"Then there will be no one to hear you screa—" Oh. Wrong story (*five points if you can name the movie*).

Just kidding. He said, "Yes, yes, fifteen kilometers," and we were praying he really did know and wasn't just making something up like the culturally polite thing to do.

Pulling into the gas station made me second guess needing to use the restroom. I can squat in the sagebrush, no problem! There were, no exaggeration, at least fifty cars piled into this little gas station parking lot with a line waiting to get inside. I did NOT want to get out of the car anymore. In the bigger city, we can kind of blend in (until we open our mouths and speak). In the middle of nowhere, we were clearly foreigners. I hate drawing attention to myself. Pregnant ladies do NOT leave their house in Turkey, so I'm already a social pariah who sticks out (pun intended). Julie said she'd go with me, and we bravely headed in towards the restroom. This is where the fun began.

The hallway was jam-packed with people because apparently everyone needed to relieve themselves. In order to not stick out more than I do, I tried to be polite and wait my turn, but there didn't seem to be a line into the bathroom. So we kind of inched our way in there and at first, I could only see the sinks...and the women with their feet in the sinks washing them. What in the??! We stared blankly trying to figure out what was going on. (Note that this is when my nervous giggling started). *What is happeningggg!? Why are they washing their feet? Maybe to be clean to say mid-day prayers?* (Note to self—find and buy hand sanitizer instead.)

We come around the corner a little more and...have you seen the movie *I Am Legend*? With Will Smith? Remember the scene where he sees all the zombies kind of standing and swaying in this dark room? OK, yes, you're with me now. Yes, that's exactly what the scene looked like. I'm not kidding. There were four stalls and no less than sixty to seventy women trying to get into the stalls. No one was talking or making any noise. Just this slow pushing and pulling and swaying. I looked at Julie like, "Are we really here? Is this really happening?" I giggled some more, but it was more like a nervous-hyperventilating-suppressed giggle. Like a growl and a snort. We were already a spectacle because we were clearly the only foreigners there and because we were the only ones not covering. I looked down at the sopping wet floor, really hoping that it was just water, and said a prayer of gratitude that I was wearing my tennis shoes instead of my normal flip-flops.

Julie looked at me and said, "I'm taller than any of them. We are going to just push our way up there and I *will* get you in the stall, mama." Remember in *The Princess Bride* when Andre the Giant just started pushing people out of his way and then yelled, "Everybody MOVE!" and they all stepped out of his way so Wesley could get through?" Yeah, it didn't happen like that, but that's what I envisioned when she said she was going to push her way up to the front. Instead, she just moshed and pushed and pulled until we were close. When the occupant started to open the door, the poor woman couldn't even get out without four women trying to get IN first. As soon as the next door "unlocked" and the occupant started walking out, Julie shoved me in front of her and kept pointing to my belly to anyone that tried to beat me in there first. She slammed the door behind me and stood guard outside.

Once safely in the stall, I caught my breath and looked around giggling. Dangit. No toilet. Just the porcelain hole in the ground. I expected it after my previous rude awakening—experiences with the infamous porcelain hole-in-the-ground, but sincerely hoped to be able to rest my rear in peace rather than start a session of Potty Pilates. But alas, Potty Pilates it was. No woman should ever have to squat at eight months pregnant. Using all my strength and Lamaze class breathing techniques, I finally got up. Pilates session finished...*but where's the toilet paper?* Only running water and a tiny plastic pitcher to "rinse off." Ohhhhh, oh geez. The floor. The water. The women washing their feet in the sink. The eight-inch toilet opening. It was all making sense now.

The raspy giggling started again. And the gagging...all the way back to the car.

Line of cars waiting to get into the gas station in the middle of nowhere

THE BIRTH

Turkey, September, month three

Want to know a secret? When I was young, I used to put a ball or pillow under my shirt and stand admiringly in the mirror thinking how cute I looked pregnant. During those same years of delusional thinking, I would have a recurring nightmare quite frequently in which I would dream that I was pregnant and so excited until it came time to deliver the baby and then I was terrified. In my dreams, I was running down the hospital hall away from the doctors and nurses until I found a bathroom stall to hide in. Every time I had the same thought: *I don't want to do this! How can I get this baby out without delivering it?!* Then I would wake up in a sweat and be so glad it was a dream. Not even in these recurring nightmares during childhood and adolescence would I have EVER imagined that one day when I was thirty years old and about to have my second child, I would be lying on an operating room table in the middle of Turkey, about to have a C-section.

I sat there (mostly) naked on the operating room table with tears streaming down my face. I kept smiling at everyone and saying, "*Çok üzgünüm.Çok üzgünüm* (I'm so sorry. I'm so sorry)." I couldn't stop crying. I wanted to be this happy, friendly American and show that I could do this! I had already had a C-section before, so I knew what to expect, but the tears came as soon as they took Aaron (who also happens to be my translator) away while they prepared me for surgery. I felt like I was having an out-of-body experience and while I sat there trying to control my hormones, every time someone said something to me in Turkish, I cried harder. I couldn't understand anything that all six people in the room were saying. I felt so very naked, far away from home and my comfort zone. I could tell all the nurses and doctors were trying to comfort me, but all I heard was a language I didn't understand and I was putting mine and my baby's life in their hands. To control my hysterics they gave me a sedative and I fought so hard to stay awake to see our little girl when she arrived. *"Çok üzgünnnnn..."*

The next thing I knew, my eyes were fluttering open and Aaron was beside me stroking my face and kissing my forehead. In my head, I asked him if the baby was here yet, but I couldn't quite form the words. Somehow he seemed to understand what my eyes were saying because he responded with, "She's almost here, babe. You're doing great." Then I was gone again.

I came to again when the room erupted in gentle cheers and clapping as everyone welcomed our sweet Ayla into the world.

"Hoşgeldiniz, Ayla!" Welcome Ayla!

"Maşallah!" God willed it!

"Çok tatlı!" So sweet!

Remember when I said children are worshiped here? There is a reverence for children as if they are sacred beings. If I leave with nothing else from Turkey, I will be forever grateful to have witnessed such a beautiful welcome to a brand new baby.

The anesthesiologist had our video camera and was recording for us, while a nurse had our camera and was taking pictures. Everyone in the room was happy and celebrating like it was their own family member and the first time they'd ever seen a baby born.

I was able to see Ayla and kiss her before I was out of it again. Whatever they were giving me was amazingggg. Like *Alice in Wonderland,* amazing.

Now. When moving overseas, one is confronted with cultural differences all the time. That is expected. The thing is, those differences are like ninjas and present themselves at times when you're least expecting it. You have NO idea when the next one will jump out and present itself.

The next thing I remember after the *Alice* drugs was waking up to someone massaging my breasts. Literally. Massagggggging my breasts. How could I NOT remember this? I first looked at the hands and then slowly looked up at a young girl in scrubs who said something to me which I can only assume meant something like, "I'm helping your milk come in." For all I knew she was saying, "I don't even work here!" A little uncomfortable, but whatever.

When they finally brought Ayla into me and I was able to hold her, I noticed that she still had all the birth stuff on her. Having already had a baby in the States, the first thing they do is wipe the baby off and make them all clean and baby-like. So when they handed her to me I was NOT expecting to see her bloody and crusty. When Aaron asked the nurse, they said they don't bathe the baby until either the third day—or the twentieth!? When the third day arrived, I was so excited Ayla could get her first bath.

Now, mind you, in the States, it's a very gentle process while holding your baby near a faucet and sponging them down gently with the never-failing Johnson & Johnson Baby Shampoo. Well, that is not exactly how it went. Ninja strikes again. Mom and I sat there horrified and gasping as the two older Turkish nurses stripped Ayla down and submerged her in a long rectangular tub of water (almost like a tall trash can) and then flipped her UPSIDE DOWN and dunked her again. I couldn't move because I still had the epidural attached to my spine (with a handy little clicker button to give me more *Alice in Wonderland* any time I needed), so I was practically yelling at Mom to stop them. However, the nurses were so nice and just cooed at Ayla while proclaiming *Maşallah* over and over again. Mom looked like a little child trying to decide whether or not to touch a hot stove—hesitantly reaching her hand out, pulling it back, reaching out, pulling back.

At what point do you offend the other culture because of your own culture? Where is that magical line? When do you forgo your own in order to respect the other? THIS is the question I've asked myself over and over again.

I was traumatized, but Ayla was finally clean and swaddled with enough blankets to withstand a polar vortex when they handed her back to me. She was understandably still fussing after being through her dunk tank experience, so I gave her a binky to help soothe her. Wrong move. The ninja cultural difference strikes again! The sweet Turkish nurse came over and as lovingly as she could, plucked the binky right out of Ayla's mouth. Shocked, I looked up at her as she said something with a twinkling smile and then walked out. What had I done wrong?! We pulled out another binky, plopped it right back in her mouth, and soon all three of us (my mom, Ayla, and I) were asleep. When we woke up, Ayla's binky was gone—again! Never mind—we brought plenty from home and just got out a new one. When the third binky went missing we called Aaron, who was at home with Will, and asked if he could speak to one of the nurses for us and ask what had happened. After listening to Aaron and the nurse's conversation in Turkish, the nurse handed the phone back to me and quickly walked out of the room. Aaron explained that Turks strongly discourage the use of binkies because they believe it can prevent the baby from being able to nurse properly. A few minutes later the nurse came back laughing and handed us our pile of binkies. That was the first of many, many times I've used the phrase, "*Uh, biz yabancıyız* (Um, we're foreign)" while shrugging. It has become my magical go-to phrase to help justify and explain many of my foreign actions and somehow give me a "hall pass" to behave in a way that normally may be culturally unacceptable.

Later while packing up to go home with Ayla (in a taxi nonetheless) the staff brought us one more meal. Being that this hospital was a private hospital—think The Four Seasons when I'm used to a Holiday

Inn—the meals were tailored to each person individually. The new mothers received foods that would help their milk come in and not cause gas, while the men received normal meals. Not only was it prepared for each patient, but it was *almost* Michelin Star–worthy. Either that or I was still in Wonderland.

This birth experience was already unforgettable, but our experience arriving home really sealed the deal for me. We pulled up in a taxi and Mustafa Bey was standing there waiting for us with a single rose in his hand. He hobbled over to us, grinning his toothless grin, and shouted, "*Hoşgeldin*, Ayla! (Welcome, Ayla!)." After handing me the rose, he took out something from his pocket and pinned it to Ayla's car seat. It was a little Evil Eye to "ward off the evil spirits."

I love this country!

THE PRESCHOOL

T*urkey, October, month four*
      Do you want to know what costs more than college tuition? An international preschool in Turkey, that's what. My sanity is at stake, though, and you can't put a price on that. I realized I reached my limit when I walked around the corner and saw Will in the bathroom, standing on top of the washing machine, trying to "aim" into the toilet. He missed. Everywhere. I realized we needed some structure, so Will started preschool this week and we (Will and I) couldn't be happier. We still don't have a car yet, so they send a bus to pick him up. A BUS! For my two-year-old. I still have difficulty with the concept of putting my two-year-old on a bus in a foreign country and sending him to school, but he loves it.

The other day, while I was putting him on the bus, I tried to make small talk with the bus monitor. Read: If the bus monitor likes me, she'll like my son and take better care of him. You see how this works? So I said in a mixture of English and what little Turkish I know, "*Gunaydin*! (Good morning!) Oh, your sweater is *Çok güzel*! (So cute!)."

"Tank you. You know what is? Tee bucks," she said with a smile on her face, feeling proud of her sweater. I noted the inability to say the -TH sound, which does not exist in the Turkish language.

"Three Bucks! That's amazing! Where did you get it?"

"Tee bucks. Yes."

"Yes, three bucks! That's amazing! But WHERE did you get it. *Nerede??* (Where?)." I said slower for her. Bless her heart.

"Madame, tee bucks in Kizilay Mall."

"Ohhh the mallllll. What storrrrre?" I said, speaking even slower and shrugging my shoulders exaggeratedly so she could understand I was asking a question.

"Madame. SEEEE?" she says, slowing down for *me*. Then she grabs the back of her shirt and pulls it around to the front and points to the tag that says, T-BOXX. "Is a store. In Kizilay Mall."

Soooo awesome. Well, this is going to be fun, isn't it?

Yesterday, the preschool had a Halloween party and someone forgot to tell the Turks that it's JUST Halloween. Somehow they missed the memo that kids normally just dress up and say trick-or-treat. I think because it's an international preschool and they cater to Americans, they want to really respect our holidays and impress parents, so they treated it like the Golden Globes. It was a h-u-g-e event. Not only did the school hire a videographer, but some parents brought their own personal photographers as well. Didn't we look like fools when we showed up in jeans and sandals, carrying our own cameras. In the midst of all the yelling, I kept hearing the same word over and over again. *Peynir! Peynir!* Recognizing this as the Turkish word for "cheese," I realized they were trying to get their kids to smile for the photos. Someone please explain the concept behind why we say, "chEEse" when we're having our picture taken. They just took the idea and translated the word without even realizing *why* that word is said in the first place. I bet all of their pictures end up looking like they're growling...or trying to be pirates. It's OK though, because they all look like a million bucks. We missed that memo. The Turkish parents showed up in suits and dresses with their best jewelry on and hair done. I'm not kidding. For years to come, I will be in the background of a picture in some Turkish photo album looking like I'm on my way to volunteer at the local animal shelter rather than celebrating Halloween Turkish style at the International (University-Level Expensive) Preschool Golden Globes.

THE CHARADES—PART I

T urkey, November, month five
Before moving overseas, we heard every recommendation for foods to try, places to visit, acceptable areas to live in, and the best language books to use. What NOBODY suggested was to brush up on our charades game skills, because living overseas is just one giant guessing game. It's like stripping every layer of pride you have and making a fool of yourself in front of complete strangers. My dignity has been tested in ways I didn't think possible.

Charades is all fun and games when you're asking for things like the restroom, a drink, or the telephone, but that's novice level. I advanced to the intermediate level when I was faced with needing binkies, a screwdriver, toddler pull-ups, and WD-40, or whatever the Turkish equivalent is. I must have passed, because I was thrust into the expert round of charades and I. Did. Not. Succeed. I had my charades game handed to me on a platter and fell flat on my face.

On one such occasion, I had just had Ayla. I had prepared for everything before our move except for stocking up on nursing pads, and I had no idea where to find them. Unfortunately, Target has not built any stores in Turkey. I went to the biggest grocery store and found the baby section, but after spending twenty minutes looking with no luck, I finally flagged down a female employee. I was hoping it would be less awkward to play "nursing pad charades" with a female in this extremely conservative country.

"*Var mi*....?? (Is there....??)" and this is when the charades began. But first, stop and ask yourself how on earth you would make the gesture for nursing pads?

Seriously.

Stop reading.

Ask yourself how you would do it, because I do not want judgments when I explain how I did it.

At first, I avoided eye contact and just made circles with my hands in the chest region. Then, when that didn't work, I proceeded by pretending to rock a baby. In my mind, they could clearly see that a baby was crying and hungry and my milk was coming in. It was so obvious. Nope, still nothing. This time I made eye contact and tried to telepathically send signals that I hoped translated to "n-u-r-s-i-n-g p-a-d-s." Finally, I made a little hook with my finger. Yes, like a child pretending to be Captain Hook. The hook was clearly portraying leaking breast milk. I put it up to my chest and with my other hand I slapped and covered the hook, like it was a nursing pad stopping the leaking milk.

No, I'm not kidding.

I was still met with blank stares and she held up a finger and said, "*Bir dakika*," which I knew must mean "one minute." I stayed put planning my escape route when a male walked up with his female co-worker. He asked me in English (hallelujah) how he could help me. I said, "Oh, thank heavens. Do you have any nursing pads?" Unfortunately, he must not have learned English vocabulary associated with pregnancy and nursing because he just said, "Sorry, I am not understand. Could you repeat?" For the love of humanity! *Sir, if you did not understand the first time, I promise you won't understand the second.* So this time I said very slowly, "Do. You. Have. Any. Nursing. Pads?" while making the same Captain Hook gesture, but making the hook come out my collar bone to avoid drawing his attention to my engorged chest region. That probably really confused him. Imagine some foreign lady making a hook with her finger that is coming out of her neck and expecting them to guess what I need. Uggggh. I ended up just saying, "*Önemli değil* (It isn't important)" and walked away.

Humble Pie: 10. Dignity: 0.

It took a few days, but I finally discovered they sell nursing pads at the PHARMACY, because why wouldn't nursing pads be with all the medicine? The pharmacist spoke English and knew exactly what they were. I was mentally exhausted by this particular charade game and so grateful for it to be over.

THE RIVER

Turkey, November, month five

If I were to use the verbs screaming, gasping, flinching, and growling, which activity do you think I was doing? If you guessed MMA fighting, you'd be incorrect, but close. Driving—in Turkey to be more precise. I feel that it's physically impossible to not make any noise when driving here.

Our car finally arrived and, anxious to have some freedom back, I immediately went to a bigger grocery store, but not without seeing my life flash before my eyes several times. Someone described the driving here like "a river" and it just flows and the only rules are whoever gets there first, wins. My problem is that I'm a rule follower and that doesn't work when there aren't any rules. The only rule that does seem to apply is that pedestrians do NOT have the right-of-way. It doesn't matter if you're ninety years old or nine months pregnant, if you don't move fast enough, they will not slow down.

I've tried to practice the "river" method of driving, but it's impossible when trying to also follow GPS. You can't read the street signs, because they are the size of 4x6 index cards. With twelve-point font. In a foreign language.

Don't get me started on the traffic lights. I need to take a driving course just to understand the lights. They have the normal red, yellow, and green lights, but there are all sorts of funny little tricks with the lights. Their green lights start blinking to warn you before even turning yellow, which definitely throws me off. Then it blinks yellow and then red. THEN there is a countdown clock above the red light counting down before it blinks yellow AGAIN and then green. I'm surprised they don't have a flashing blue light or something to warn you that it's going to count down and then blink red before it turns yellow before it turns green. What's funny is that as soon as it starts blinking yellow before turning green, everyone just goes. No one waits until it's green. Like I said before, don't follow the rules, just follow the flow.

Obviously, I have messed up the flow a few times, but it's almost like they know I'm foreign. I wave to say "thank you" and they just blink their eyes tightly shut. I found myself involuntarily responding the same way and just felt stupid. It's like seeing someone wink at you and it's just an automatic reaction to wink back at them. Kind of awkward. (Ok, honestly—how many of you actually just tried blinking tightly like them??). Seeing this multiple times, I asked Aaron to ask someone why everyone is blinking. We've learned it's their way of saying "you're welcome."

When I don't feel brave enough to face the "river" of driving or feel like paying eleven dollars a gallon (literally), we take a taxi bus. They are mini-busses that hold up to twenty people, and they are ingenious, I tell you. You can flag one down and it will pull over and then when someone is ready to get off, they just yell a certain phrase. I have yet to decipher what that phrase is, so I wait until someone else does, but that usually results in me needing to walk farther.

This is all new to me and I'm taking driving day by day. Aaron, on the other hand, is living his boyhood dream of racing every day and weaving in and out of cars. It's like a real-life video game and I'm just along for the ride.

THE FULL NELSON

C *yprus, November, month five*
Either admirably or stupidly, we took our two-year-old and two-month-old on vacation over Thanksgiving break to visit Cyprus. What better way to celebrate the Native Americans and the Pilgrims coming together peacefully than to visit the Greeks and Turks in Cyprus with a newborn and toddler, right?

Half of it was a blur because we were exhausted to the point of it almost being considered inhumane torture (Ayla doesn't sleep particularly well). With our bloodshot eyes and delusions, we kept going. *Must travel. Must not let kids slow us down. This is...amazing?*

We thought that we could either be exhausted at home or exhausted on a Mediterranean island, so we chose the latter, duh. When we arrived at our hotel, it was like walking onto the set of *My Big Fat Greek Wedding* except they were Turks. The *abla* and *abi* who owned the place practically fell all over Aaron when he started speaking Turkish to them. That was until they saw the kids. As you recall, it is literally in the Turkish blood to fawn all over children. Children are born celebrities and they can do no wrong. The sweet owners immediately took the kids from our arms and practically danced around the room with them, kissing them and shoving candies in Will's mouth.

After being shown to our room, we could barely keep our eyes open and immediately got ready for bed. I fed Ayla and laid her in the middle of our bed, while Aaron got Will ready for bed in the adjacent room. Will was having a difficult time going to sleep because of all the "whitning and funder" outside. The *abla* had told us that there was supposed to be a storm and to expect it to rain all night. Add that to the list of *Ways to Torture Exhausted Parents*. I quickly brushed my teeth in the bathroom and avoided the mirror and my bloodshot eyes all while making a mental note of how many hours I had before Ayla would wake up hungry again. After turning off the lights except for a small night light, I crawled into bed next to Ayla, feeling as giddy as a child on Christmas morning to be able to finally go to sleep. After my eyes adjusted I noticed how porcelain my baby girl's face looked—almost like it was glistening. *I made that little porcelain human*, I thought dreamily. *Wait. She looks TOO porcelain. She looks like glass in this dim light*. It looked so out of place that I turned on the lights once again to get a better look.

She didn't look like glass—she looked wet! My adrenaline starting to kick in, I looked all around her trying to figure out why her face looked wet. I finally looked up and that's when I saw tiny bubbles in the ceiling and water starting to drip faster and faster directly onto my baby's head.

"Aaron!" I whisper-yelled. "Aaron, the ceiling is leaking!" I picked Ayla up and moved her because the water drops seemed to be using her face as a target for landing practice. I ran to yank off Aaron's eye mask and pull out his earplugs. Will must have been in that foggy, in-between state that happens just after falling asleep, because he woke up when I came in and just started crying. Aaron jumped out of bed and looked around the room in a distorted haze and when he finally came to, he tried to call the front office, but they weren't answering the phones. I ran back into my room and saw that the ceiling bubbles had doubled in size and number. As the storm raged on both outside and now inside too, I just yelled to Aaron that I was going to run down to the front office to try and get our room moved. We were on the second floor of a two-story hotel and I ran to the end of the hall to the landing where the stairs were but stopped dead in my tracks. The first floor was a river of water. Lightning and thunder were happening simultaneously. I just started deliriously cackling at this point. I kept thinking, *This is why sleep deprivation is used as a torture device. It slowly makes you go crazy to the point of cackling.*

Back in the room, I told Aaron all hope was lost. This is it. This is the end. The hotel is flooding and the ceiling is melting and I'm losing brain cells by the minute. Actually...he had called the front desk and they were on their way up to help us change rooms, but at that point, I was in my alternate reality saying my goodbyes.

Abi did in fact come up, and the poor man was beside himself. It hadn't rained that hard in "over forty years," he said. Their hotel had never flooded or leaked before. After seeing the ceiling bubbles, he moved us across the hall to another room with only two leaking ceiling bubbles because apparently the roof was leaking everywhere and the first floor was flooded.

I don't know if I really slept that night. I don't know if any of us did, but it eventually stopped raining and the sun came out and the birds were chirping at an ungodly hour. I zombie-walked across the hall with Ayla in my arms and somehow managed to get dressed.

When I heard a knocking sound, I didn't know if it was my headache banging in my head or the door to our room. I opened it up to find *abla* and *abi* standing there asking me something in Turkish with sorrowful smiles on their faces. I ran to get Aaron so he could speak with them, but when we came back into my room from the adjoining room, both *abla* and *abi* were already inside and coo-ing at Ayla. She had just started smiling the week before and she was on full display that morning. (She is truly the most beautiful baby, with feathery eyelashes and almond eyes.)

Abla abruptly said something to Aaron and before he could respond or before I knew what was happening, *abla* grabbed Ayla and flipped my new baby over and was performing a Full Nelson on her! I gasped and lunged, but not before she grabbed Ayla's right arm behind her back and attached it to her left leg and popped every bone in her body. Ob-vi-ous-ly Ayla was crying at this point, but the sweet *abla* had such a pleasant smile on her face and waved me away like she knew what she was doing. I'm not one for confrontation and stopped in my tracks with hands stretched out like I was unsure of what to do. Aaron was nervously speaking Turkish to her and telling her that I was worried about my baby and maybe she should stop. She *tsked* at me kindly with a wrinkled wink (Can you even *tsk* kindly? How is that possible?), waving me back again, and I watched in horror as she performed a version of the Boston Crab on her.

Now, I must say, I have never seen a wrestling match in my life. I don't even know if it's called a match, a game, or a meet. The only terms I've ever heard in my life are "body slam" and "drop kick," but in order to properly tell this story and give a visual, I spent a good amount of time looking up terms for the actions I saw on my poor two-month-old baby. My Google searches went something like this:

-ARM AND LEG DIAGONAL YOGA WRESTLING TERM
-BODY PINNED HEAD UP AND ARMS OUT WRESTLING TERM
-TURKISH CUSTOM TERM CRACKING BABY BONES

As soon as she was done, *abla* stepped proudly back with a gleaming smile on her face, proud of the service she had just performed for us. *Abi* stood proudly behind his wife resting his hands on her hard-worked shoulders. She told Aaron that she was stretching Ayla's joints and hips so that she will sleep well and be relaxed. Although I was horrified beyond belief, I felt a sense of appreciation for this sweet woman, with her hair tied up in a scarf, sharing her knowledge of wrestling babies that she had probably performed on her own children or grandchildren and that was probably performed on her as an infant. I doubt she had ever pinned any other guest's baby, but we were special because we (Aaron) spoke Turkish and therefore she trusted us enough to share part of her cultural tradition with us.

I prayed that Ayla wasn't permanently damaged and that I would trust that hundreds of other Turkish babies had the same thing done to them and they're all fine now. I literally don't remember what else we did that day and I only remember only a handful of things we did on that trip, but I will never forget seeing my baby in the arms of a kind-hearted Turkish woman in a Full Nelson.

THE HOLIDAYS

Turkey, January, month seven

Besides unwittingly being a part of the WWF, the rest of our Cyprus vacation was perfect. We spent time on both the Turkish side and the Greek side. For those not familiar with Cyprus, there is literally a line that is in the middle of the island that divides the Turks in the north from the Greeks in the south. Not unlike the line my sister and I used to draw in the middle of the sheets when we shared a bed, not to be crossed or touched. We each had our "own space." So after we'd spent time in the north, the taxi driver dropped us off at the border with all our luggage, car seats, and belongings. We walked the 100 yards alone in "no man's land" before reaching the tiny little passport shack on the Greek side and then on to the taxis.

Years ago, Aaron had lived in Cyprus and part of the reason for this trip was to see people he knew. We planned to go to church and surprise many of the people, but upon arrival at the church, we found it locked and closed. Ayla was screaming and wanting to be fed and Will needed a diaper change. We would need to walk three blocks back to the main street to get a taxi. Feeling overwhelmed, we just sat down on the steps trying to come up with a plan. All of a sudden an older man came out of his house across the street and yelled something in Greek to Aaron. I was worried because it was clear we were not Greek Orthodox and I was unsure how they would react towards us. I froze and looked straight to the ground. This sweet man and his wife had seen us with fussing children, and now they invited us to their house to get water for a bottle and a place to change Will. I cannot even begin to tell you the gratitude I felt for this sweet older couple as they fed us and let us stay for an hour while getting our bearings. Will played with their grandson's toys, and as we were leaving, they gave us the little Greek singing toy he had been playing with. I don't think I'll ever be able to part with it.

After returning to Turkey after Thanksgiving, I was so homesick and missing the good ol' US of A. The holiday season was just making it worse because Turkey is 99 percent Muslim, meaning they don't celebrate Christmas and the only upcoming holiday was New Years. We already missed Thanksgiving and then knowing I would miss Christmas, I was questioning the very meaning of life. No, not really...but I wanted to be hearing Christmas songs playing in the stores and seeing the stores display all the Christmas magic. No, none of that here. On the bright side, however, they *do* play Christmas songs every now and again, but it's usually in Turkish movies. Yes, they use songs like "Carol of the Bells" during their fast-action sequences in thriller movies. No one told them it's a Christian Christmas song. Brings a smile to my face.

Our church also had a Christmas party, for which I was so grateful. We parked down the street from the church building and started making our way there. On the street was a construction site, and I'm sure Will thought that was his Christmas present because he loves all things with wheels. Will was so excited to see the dump truck. He waved, and we continued walking. When I noticed Will wasn't behind me anymore, I turned around and saw that he was sitting on the lap of the driver *in* the dump truck...OF COURSE he was sitting in the dump truck. Why wouldn't a two-year-old be in the dump truck? Only in Turkey. I loved it and more importantly, Will loved it. The man had seen Will so happy and yelled to him, "*Gel! Gel!* (Come! Come!)" and motioned for Will to crawl up into the dump truck with him. He literally stopped his job to let a little child crawl up in the dump truck. All that was missing was the jolly laugh and the big white beard.

Our little family Christmas dinner turned into the United Nations Christmas at the Cardways'. We invited a few people and it snowballed into a huge group. We had people who were refugees and had nowhere to go or individuals who were the only Christians in their families and had no one to celebrate Christmas with. In all, we had five Americans, one Turk, two Iraqis, one Tanzanian, six Iranians, and two Romanians. It was a beautiful Christmas and so much fun to hear all the languages floating around.

After everyone left, all of the emotions I had been feeling for a month, coupled with a new baby, sleepless nights, and hormones, completely exploded and I cried for two hours straight. Not the pretty cry. The ugly, snotty one. The one where my eyes were swollen shut the next morning. That is the point we decided to hire a part-time babysitter. Meet Yeliz. My instant best friend. She is my age and a single mom and I'm starting to realize how much I needed her company and friendship more than the actual help.

We have fallen into this "co-parenting" relationship, which is amazing, given the fact that she only speaks Turkish. You'd think that it might be interesting at times with the language barrier, but it hasn't been. What has been amusing, though, is the cultural barriers. The other day I asked her to take Ayla outside for some Vitamin D while I ran an errand. She looked like I just stun-gunned her. It was fifty degrees, mind you. Seeing the look on her face and knowing what she was thinking, I said, "It's OK. You can even put on her snowsuit." (Which is absurd, I think.) She shook her head and told me it was too cold and too early for a baby to go outside. I asked her when it was OK to take a baby outside and she said, "A few months." *Ha! Are you kidding me?* I started laughing, thinking she was joking, but she said, "I didn't take my son outside for the first year. It's not good for children." Clearly, we have a different mindset. She wouldn't budge and I ended up taking Ayla out myself. So funny. Turks give kids chocolate like it's water and let them ride around on the dashboard of the car, but they scold us for taking children out in fifty-degree weather (or for letting Will wear shoes in the house because "shoes give Will diseases from the street.")

I can totally see where they're going with this, but it's a bit extreme in my foreign opinion.

THE MARKET

Turkey, January, month seven
Take this lesson from me. Never assume you're being complimented in a foreign language unless you're 1,000 percent sure. And even then, proceed with caution.

At one of our many weekly visits to the market, we ran into the owner. She's not there all the time, so when we do see her, it's like running into an auntie you haven't seen in a while. An auntie who is ninety-five pounds, with a cigarette glued to her fingers and smoker's voice deeper than James Earl Jones. I hadn't seen her since I had Ayla, which is over three months now. Ayla was at home napping with Yeliz, but I was so excited to show her pictures of the baby.

"*Merhaba*!! Hello!! I had the baby!" I proclaimed in English and with what little Turkish I knew while pointing to my belly. "Uh, *bebek!*" I pretended to rock an invisible baby. "Look...*Bak*...here's the picture of our little girl," I said while pulling out my phone to show her a picture of Ayla.

"*Sldkgjglkhjgjhsljksl,fdmshdgoiy,*" she said, because really, that's all it sounds like to me. I assumed she understood what I said and was asking the normal questions one asks when someone has a baby.

"Yes! Here she is! Her name is Ayla. *Onun adi Ayla.*"

"*Lksjdgskdjghsiguosigy,*" she said, smiling and patting my stomach.

"Haha, thank you! I still have a ways to go. I gained a lot of weight this pregnancy," I said bashfully and then motioned "BIG" with my arms to help her understand my English.

"*Kljgdfglkdjgsoiuss*??"

Not understanding why she looked confused or what she said, I called over to Aaron, who was talking to someone else in Turkish and asked him to come translate. Aaron then turned to her and presumably explained that I hadn't understood and to repeat what she had said.

"*Kljgdfglkdjgsoiuss*??"

"What did she say, Aaron?" I asked, but he ignored me and responded to her, "*ldkgjdfoiguoiaywfjbeneboikgu.....*"

"*LIKJDGBSOIDUGSD!!*" she exclaimed and patted my tummy again.

"AARON—what is she saying??!"

"Uh, she's excited..."

"BUT WHAT DID SHE SAY?"

"Um, she wants to know when the baby is due."

OH. Awesome.

THE SISTERS—PART II

T*urkey, February, month eight*
Remember our neighbors? The sisters? Well, they're full of advice and apparently I need it. I'm not sure if it's the "neighborly" thing to do in Turkey or if I'm such a hot mess that it's necessary. Here is some of the advice I was given this week:

Belgin: Alicia, you must breastfeed Ayla. If you do, she will crawling by four months and her teeth will coming at four and half months. Is true.

Bilge: You must not let Will go without socks or house slippers. He will catch pneumonia.

Me: Oh it's OK. Americans go barefoot all the time. We're used to it.

Bilge: No, you are in Turkey, he must wear socks.

Belgin: Will, do you want some chocolate?

Me, interjecting: Oh, no thank you. Will, say, "No thank you." He can't have any more sugar today.

Belgin: Here, Will, have little chocolate.

Me: No, seriously. Will, look at Mommy. Look at my eyes—don't you dare. *(Turning to the sisters)* Please, he won't sleep tonight if he has chocolate.

Belgin: Well, that's because you put him to bed too early.

They then proceeded to completely undermine me and gave Will the chocolate anyway. They shushed me away and told me I should try a 10 p.m. bedtime—and they are serious. Many Turkish parents live by the rule that the children decide when they're tired.

Remember, they have never been married, nor had children, BUT somehow they know everything about how I should be raising my kids. I totally love them and just have to take everything they say with a grain of salt. While the following is not advice, it should be recorded and served any time I should need a piece of that delicious humble pie:

Belgin: You know, Alicia, I have thinking. You are very pretty girl.

Me: *Standing a little taller and....well...beaming.* Thank you, Belgin! That's so nice of you!

Belgin: Yes. I did not very notice when you were pregnant. I could not see it.

Please stop talking.

THE CHARADES—PART II

T urkey, *February, month eight*
During this round of charades, the game in which I'm always an unsuspecting participant, I was going to the market down the street to buy meat from the butcher. While we can go to the American grocery store, it's about thirty minutes away and it's much more convenient to just walk a hundred yards to the market at the end of the street. Additionally, the local meat is much better quality and I prefer the local meat to the frozen, shipped-from-the-States options at the American grocery store. Normally I ask Yeliz to go get some things for me, but she wasn't coming for a few days and so I decided to brave it.

I don't have access to the internet on my phone once we leave the house so I planned out what I wanted to say and practiced it a few times before leaving. I repeated the phrase under my breath the entire way to the market. When I arrived, I felt confident and proudly strode up to the tiny butcher's section. Just to put things in perspective, the market is about the same size as a gas station lobby. It has your necessities along with a small produce and butcher section.

"*Tavuk istiyorum lütfen* (I want chicken, please)," I asked the stone-faced butcher. Normally, I get some sort of smile when I have my children with me, but this man was NOT breaking character.

"Which part?" he mumbled without even looking up. Oh. Huh? I wasn't prepared for a response and had no idea what he just said.

"Sorry. I don't understand. I'm learning Turkish. I'm foreign," I said in Turkish. (My memorized go-to phrase during every conversation).

"WHICH PART?" he said again in a louder voice. I finally realized what he was asking, but I didn't know the names for the parts of the chicken. I started to panic and felt my face getting hot. I noticed the posters behind him of previous Turkish leaders and several Turkish flags. This man was clearly a nationalist, and typically nationalists did not care much for foreigners, especially ones from countries starting with Uh and ending in Merica. It also meant he was most likely a conservative Muslim, which explained his lack of eye contact with a female.

Enter: Daily Charades for 400, please.

Not wanting to offend the butcher and knowing that I had at least eighteen months left of visiting this market, I tried to play my charades cards very carefully, but no matter what body part I came up with for the chicken, I was going to lose. If I chose thighs, I'd have to point to my thighs. Lose. If I chose the neck, legs, or feet, I'd only end up making broth. Lose. What I really wanted was the white meat—the breast. You can imagine my dilemma. At first, I just looked off into the distance avoiding eye contact and made a circular motion of the trunk of my body about a foot away from myself, praying he would understand. Nope, he just looked off into the distance as well trying to figure out where I was looking. Dagnabit.

He looked back at me still avoiding eye contact. So I flattened my hands and put one perpendicular to my neck and one at my waist. Was it not obvious that I wanted the breast that was in between the two hands?! No. By this time there was a line behind me and I was royally embarrassing myself, my gender, and my country. I finally just looked down and discreetly pointed to my chest. I *pointed* to my *chest* to the angry, conservative butcher man. I was mortified and I'm sure he was too. My other hand grabbed my finger and pulled it away from my chest as if it had a mind of its own and I was not to blame. *Oh please, just let this end. Can I tap my heels three times? There's no place like home. There's no place like home.* Nope, still there. This time he was holding up two breasts (how ironic) and asking me something that I thought was "How many breasts?." I shamefully held up four fingers and grabbed the good-for-nothing meat. As I was walking away, out of the corner of my eye, I saw him break character and wink and coo at my two-year-old.

I bought frozen meat for the next three months or asked Yeliz to pick some up for me before I showed my face to him again.

THE BANK

Turkey, March, month nine
  Note to self. Always be prepared—and when I say "prepared," I mean showered, teeth brushed, and somewhat presentable. Saturday morning we decided to go for a walk with the kids. We made our way towards a park and saw a group of people photographing two boys dressed in full costume. I wondered what was happening and why they were dressed like Ottoman princes. I've since seen a dozen or so and they're all chauffeured around in nicely decorated cars like a wedding. I learned that these little princes are celebrating their *Sunnet,* which is a ritual that marks the transition from boyhood to manhood. Basically, they're about to be "snip, snipped." The *Sunnet* is a circumcision party. After watching and admiring this foreign tradition, we made our way back home.

We were rounding the corner by the bank at the end of our street when my buddy, the security guard, the same one that carried screaming Will when I was pregnant, came running out of the bank. He was excited to see us as usual, but especially because Aaron was with us and he could speak with him. Will lit up when he saw him and stuck out his hand for a candy with a big smile on his face. The guard just laughed and laughed, "Praise God! I could eat you! Num num num!"

Then the guard got so excited, like he just had the best idea, and asked, "You want tea?!"

"Oh no, but thank you so much! That is so kind of you," Aaron responded while placing his hand over his chest (the polite, cultural way of indicating "No, thank you").

"No, please. Come for tea. Come. Come. Come," and then he grabbed Will's hand and just started walking into the bank. So into the bank we went.

I was in sweats, mind you. With no makeup and a messy bun. Not the cute messy bun—the ugly, greasy one. Saturdays are for relaxing—not for looking pretty. Banks around here are high class. The women who work there go to get "blowouts" each morning before work. Slightly embarrassed, we walked in and the guard immediately directed us up the stairs. All the perfectly coiffed ladies were squealing at the children and handing us candy while repeating the phrase "*Maşallah*" over and over again. "Praise God! Praise God!"

At the top of the stairs, the guard led us down a long hallway and into the corner office with floor-to-ceiling windows overlooking the city. He sat us down and left to go and get the tea. While he was gone a very professional and impeccably dressed man walked into the room. He said something to Aaron to which Aaron started firing off rapid Turkish. I could tell Aaron was a little nervous by the way he was laughing. So by default, I got really nervous and started laughing. You know, like sympathy laughter.

Aaron turned to me quickly and said under his breath, "This is the President of the bank and this is his office. He didn't know he had guests today."

Awkward.

The guard came back and acted like it's totally normal to bring a random, foreign family into your boss's office for tea. Five minutes later we were all having tea together and overlooking the city. In Turkey, when children are present, everyone is happy.

THE GYM

T*urkey, March, month nine*
You never see runners here. In all the months we've been here I've seen two the entire time, and that says something because we are out a lot. We see casual walkers, but not people exercising. After I had Ayla, I wanted to start exercising again, but was afraid to run for fear of, what, being the only runner? Every day I pass this sign on the way to the park that says *Club Spor*, so I was eager to check it out. Translating beforehand everything I needed to ask, I gained the courage to go and inquire about a membership. I walked up to the door and it was completely shaded and covered, yet I had just seen someone come out of there so I knew it was open. Feeling really awkward, I snooped around the building a bit to see if I could look in one of the windows. My assumption was that because gyms and sports clubs are not common here, they covered the windows to protect everyone's privacy and modesty. I was also aware that the window coverings might be the ones where the insiders can see out, but the outsiders can't see in, like a two-way mirror, so I was hesitant to stick my face against the window and try to see in. I could only imagine all the exercisers laughing while watching this woman carrying a baby on a back sling and holding a toddler's hand trying to see inside. No, that was not the way to go, I decided. Looking down the length of the building, I saw a window open. I casually strolled down past the window, hoping to be as inconspicuous as possible, and strained my neck and squinted my eyes to get a good look inside. Do you know what I saw? It was not an elliptical, I'll tell you that! It was a bed. Idiot! I quickly ran back

towards the door and down the sidewalk away from the building and thanked my lucky stars I didn't walk in there with my kids in tow. It was a brothel. Yep.

I decided sports clubs and brothels were not the way to go, so I started running outdoors, even though I was the only one. The first time I ran in the neighborhood, I startled some older gentlemen standing by the market. They looked at me and jumped and then looked in the direction I was running and THEY started to quickly head that direction too like, *she must be running from something, so we should start running too!* I passed them and they were still looking around so confused and then they just stared and I swear they were thinking, "*She is flat out of her mind.*" But it's OK because that was what I was thinking the entire time too.

THE SISTERS—PART III

T urkey, April, month ten
    As per our weekly routine, we walked across the hall to see
our cute neighbors, the single sisters, Belgin and Bilge. As usual, they
offered Will some chocolate. Here is exactly how the conversation
went:

"Will, you want some chocolate? Mom, may you permit him some
chocolate?" Bilge asked.

"No, but thank you for asking! He has already had sweets today
and he shouldn't have any more." (I was elated they actually asked this
time. We were making progress!)

"*Slgkjfgidoigfudkfgdflkgjldfjgldkgj.*" They were rapidly speaking in
Turkish to each other. One left and came back in with a simit (like a
bagel) and an entire chocolate bar on a plate. I wasn't really surprised
they did this. It happens every time.

I immediately said, "Will, you can have the simit, but not the
chocolate." *He started whining and I didn't want to deal with a
meltdown in their apartment.* "OK, only a tiny little bite. It's not good
for your tummy."

"Alicia, is he circumcised?" Belgin asked me. *I'm sorry—WHAT?* I
sat there for a split second, totally caught off guard.

"Haha! What? Um, uh, yes." I mumbled. Out of the corner of
my eye, I saw Will reaching for the chocolate. "Will, don't have that
chocolate," I said, trying to remain calm, hoping SOMEONE would
listen to me.

"Alicia is good he is circumcised. Much healthy for him and will help his intestinal problems because less bacteria down there. Is OK for him to have chocolate."

I cannot believe they just said that to me. HAHA! I was secretly dying inside and also confused, but we continued to make small talk and then...

"Alicia, how much kilo you weigh?" Belgin asks. *Oh my gosh. You've got to be kidding me. Are we doing this again? I'm still not over the circumcision question.*

"I actually don't know. I only know it in pounds. Sorry." *Why did I just say sorry?! What am I apologizing for?!*

"Hmmmm. Is OK," Bilge says as she clicks her tongue. She leaves the room and COMES BACK WITH A SCALE. Again. I'm having flashbacks to my first week here. I started laughing. A lot. Kind of hysterically. These are the same women who told me that they just now realized I was cute, but they couldn't tell when I was pregnant. The same women who made me stand on a scale at eight months pregnant and now seven months post-pregnancy.

"Come. Get on scale," Belgin said while pulling on my shirt sleeve.

"Really? Uh, no thank you. I'd kind of rather not."

"Come. Come. COME." *Definitely more a command than encouragement.* I reluctantly stood up and stepped on the scale. I don't really care how much I weigh, but just out of principle I didn't want to do it. The number displayed my weight in kilos. I have no idea what the number means and if it's good or bad.

"LKJDFJGBSDFGOISDPOIFKJOIUWABOIUGOSDM!"

They immediately started speaking to each other again and I had no idea if they were impressed or disgusted.

"Is OK," Belgin said. "You just had a baby."

I DIE.

FOR SOME UNKNOWN REASON, I stayed, and we continued to make small talk. At some point Belgin said, "Oh Alicia, we love your children. It makes us so sad when you don't come over." (I go twice a week.)

"I'm sorry. We just get busy sometimes. My children love you too."

"Will is so smart. Oh, and AYLA. She is precious. She is going to be so tall and very beautiful, just like her...DADDY."

Stunned for the third time during this visit, I snort-laughed and slowly felt my face to see if the verbal slap left a mark. "Yes, yes she will," I somehow said with a straight face. "OK, *ablas*, I need to go feed Ayla cereal and get her to bed. "

"Oh, you can leave Will here. This is his house too," Belgin said, and I was grateful to have the opportunity to have some quiet time with Ayla, so I graciously accepted. "OK, thank you so much. That's so nice of you. I will be back really soon to get him."

After getting Ayla fed and in bed, I came back about thirty minutes later to get Will so he could come and have his dinner. I walked in and saw the simit still on his plate, but the entire chocolate bar was GONE. Seeing the chocolate smeared on Will's face and knowing that I would be up with him all night because he's having stomach issues and chocolate is one of the triggers, I somehow found this all hysterical. I'm in another country and I just have to blame things on the language or cultural barrier. Believe me, I would have been throwing punches if we were in the States and if they weren't so sweet. Just kidding. Kind of. But not really.

THE ROYALS—PART II

*T**urkey, June, month thirteen***

Do you want to know what I'm getting used to? All the attention and love my children get every time we walk out of the house. Want to know what I'm *not* getting used to? My children being kissed...on the lips, by random strangers. I'm not sure what it says about us as parents when he just so willingly gives his kisses away to anyone. We meet women, men, elderly couples, and teenage boys and they all kiss Will...on the lips! I'm always gobsmacked, but here it's just what they do and it has kind of started to be endearing to me. *Kind of.* I wonder how long I need to live here before the reverence of children is completely normal to me.

I was out on a walk with the kids and I had Will in the stroller and Ayla in the Baby Bjorn carrier. We stopped on the side of the street while traffic passed and once the light turned red, allowing for pedestrians to walk, there was a bus full of uniformed, armed soldiers stopped right in front of us about three feet away. They all appeared to be between the ages of eighteen and twenty-five and not only did they all start waving and blowing kisses to Will, but when the bus started moving and driving away, they ALL had the biggest smiles on their faces with their heads turned and cranked so they could watch Will as they drove away. Will just stared back in awe while slowly whispering to himself, "Soldiers!" They genuinely love children here and I LOVE IT. Poor Will is in for a rude awakening when we go home. We recently took a trip down south and we were able to stay on the air force base in Southern Turkey. Upon arrival, we went to a restaurant on base and out front were a bunch of men in uniform waiting to be seated. Will immediately jumped out of the car and ran up to them and put his hand out (for the candy, *duh*). They didn't even notice him. Like a fly on a zebra at the watering hole. Will looked so confused and upset, and we had to distract him immediately.

On that same trip, we went to the beach famous for the castle out in the sea about 500 yards from the shore. Aaron took Ayla into the water and within minutes a couple took her from Aaron's arms and played with and kissed her for the next fifteen minutes before she was passed to someone else. Who needs a babysitter when you're in Turkey?

On the way home, we were at the airport going through security. I set Ayla down for a split second to unload everything onto the conveyor belt and turned around and she was gone. I looked around frantically and then exhaled my held breath when I saw that one of the airport security agents was holding her. Of course. Every time, without fail, one of the security people takes Ayla from my arms and passes her around. This particular time, after I went through the metal detector and got my stuff, I turned around to see another security agent a couple rows over, holding Ayla and still doing his job and conducting people through the metal detector. He wouldn't give her back to me until he could have a kiss from her.

Note to self: Teach kids about Stranger Danger back in the States, but for now, let them enjoy how it *should* be.

THE SISTERS—PART IV

Turkey, July, month thirteen

Oh, Bilge and Belgin. Our Turkish experiences wouldn't be the same with them. I can't stop laughing as I think about our weekly interactions, but this one will forever be seared into my memory.

As part of our weekly routine, we went to visit the same cute, single sisters that live across the hall. We were visiting and playing, and Will accidentally kicked Ayla's head as she crawled on the floor. She started crying really hard. Both sisters were all in a tizzy because "heaven forbid" a baby cries (babies are royalty, remember?). One sister was scrambling around trying to distract her and the other one was trying to take Ayla from my arms. Ayla just cried harder. Well, then Bilge got this brilliant idea. (Let me interject and explain how she looked in this moment. She had no makeup on and some kind of clear skin mask so her skin was plastic looking. Her hair had some sort of gel or colorant at her roots and looked a bit like she stuck her finger in an electrical socket, but she had bright red lipstick on with dangling earrings. Basically she looked like she hadn't slept in four days. She was also wearing a thin cotton dress, ahem, with nothing on underneath. It was a sight.) So anyway, she got this brilliant idea to play peek-a-boo with Ayla to distract her from crying...but the Turks say, "*Jeh-eh*!" instead of "Peek-a-boo!" So she got about six inches away from Ayla's face and then covered her own face and threw back her hands and screamed, "*JEHHHH-EHHHHH.*" She literally screamed it because she was trying to be louder than Ayla's screams. She proceeded to do this four times and by this point I was laughing so hard. I wish there was a camera in the room. Ayla was crying so hard no sound was coming out, but her nostrils were just flaring and shaking. Do you get the picture? So when "*Jeh-eh*" didn't work—and I have NO idea where she got this and why she did it—she got about three inches from Ayla's face and stuck out her middle finger and flipped her off. YES. Yes—she did. Ayla stopped crying immediately like she knew what it meant and was as shocked by it as I was. Then the woman turned to her sister and said, "Works every time!"

I was completely baffled and laughing hysterically. Let me just say that I'm pretty sure she wasn't meaning to give my baby the bird, but I still have no idea where she got that from. "Works every time?" How many times has she done this?

THE HAMMAM

Turkey, *August, month fourteen*

We've done the overseas experience in a most unconventional way for Americans. Normally, the other Americans here all live near each other in the same complex. We chose to live apart from them in the hopes of having a more authentic experience. "It will be awesome," Aaron said. "You'll love it," Aaron said. I just held my breath and put my big girl pants on.

And I do love it. While it has been SO hard, it's been SO rewarding and given me so many (hilarious) experiences I would not otherwise have.

My twenty-three-year-old sister, Mia, came to visit me after being gone for eighteen months on her church mission. This was her first time overseas (with the exception of a cruise to Mexico and Jamaica), and I wanted her to have an eye-opening cultural experience. And that she did. That she did, my friends.

My Turkish friend (and our babysitter), Yeliz, invited us to go to her home village where she was raised and visit the village hammam there. A hammam is basically a public steam bath. The way it was explained to me is that these have been around for hundreds, if not thousands of years, and people would come once a week to bathe and socialize—in the nude, or mostly nude. It's a big room with floor-to-ceiling marble. There are faucets lining the walls and in the center is a giant slab of marble, raised like a table. Some of them have a little pool, while others don't. Yeliz told me it's also where women looked for and negotiated marriages for their children. It's really easy to see which girl has good child-bearing hips when she's in her birthday suit.

I was so excited to do this with Mia (and finally have someone to share my foreign experiences with) that I forgot I was dealing with the MOST modest and conservative person. This is the girl who wore oversized T-shirts and shorts from the boys' and men's sections growing up. The girl who felt naked in capped sleeves and shorts above her shins. I'm exaggerating a bit, but you get my point. This is the girl who hyperventilated and writhed on the floor like a dying worm when she first heard the birds-and-the-bees talk (and I'm not exaggerating this time.)

The day of our adventure she kept telling me she was shaking and couldn't stop her teeth from chattering because she was so nervous. "What do I wear? Where do I change? How many people will be there? I don't think I can do this," she mumbled.

I've adopted the *fake it till you make it* approach with everything overseas and encouraged her to just pretend like this *ain't no thang*. We drove out to the middle of nowhere. Truly. Nowhere. Some of the roads were paved, but most were dirt. All of the houses were cement blocks and they looked abandoned except for the clothes hanging out the windows betraying the fact that they did indeed have inhabitants. We pulled up to a small, unassuming building—a far cry from the Hilton's Hammam and Spa in the city.

By this point, Mia was shaking and starting to get the nervous giggles (it runs in the family). She turned to me and continued to babble, "I'm going to throw up. I don't think I can do this! I'll just stay in the car. Never mind, I'm coming. No, you go." We walked in and immediately were met with stares. Apparently, we don't even need to open our mouths for it to be blatantly obvious we are foreign. I blamed Mia with her blonde hair and blue eyes.

I know enough Turkish to understand that the person taking the money from Yeliz was asking who we were and why we were here.

I assume they don't get many foreigners showing up in a tiny village hammam. After paying something like six dollars, we ventured into the locker room and proceeded to change. Mia, still uncomfortable, tried changing by using a towel wrapped around herself and gaped at me when I handed her a two-piece bathing suit—like it was a piece of twine or floss. She probably had hoped for a wetsuit instead. While we were all waiting for her to shimmy out of her clothes under the towel and place the bathing suit on under her towel, I said, "Miaaaa, you're going to be nude in about five minutes, so there's no need to try and be all discreet in front of us." (We were the only ones in the locker room).

We headed to the door where the hammam was and by that point, Mia was laughing out loud and quivering uncontrollably. When we walked in, it became very quiet and all the women stopped and turned to look at us. Their previous conversations didn't resume anytime soon and they continued to all watch us silently as we walked over to set our toiletries down and claim a faucet. We were a walking spectacle. Either it was that we looked foreign or that Mia couldn't stop trying to cover herself with her arms while practically vibrating along with spurts of what I knew to be giggles while others might have assumed her throat was closing due to an allergic reaction. Either way, we'll never know why they stared.

The steam was so thick and dense. There was a pool to get into first with the purpose of soaking your skin to the point that the top layer of dead skin is wrinkled and ready to be scrubbed off. I quickly undressed (since all of the other women there had done so) and jumped in the pool.

After ten minutes, Yeliz told me that if I was ready for a scrubbing, I should go sit by the marble table and wait for the woman to come. *What woman? I thought I was scrubbing my own skin?* No sooner had I asked when the door opened and a woman came in wearing only a towel and said something to which Yeliz responded while pointing to me. Forgetting the part about "faking it till I make it," I froze. The woman looked at me with confused, impatient eyes until I reluctantly got out of the pool to make my way to the marble table —with all eyes still on me. As I walked up to the table the woman motioned for me to lie face down on the table. I was barely keeping in my nervous giggles when she gave me a wedgie with my swimsuit bottoms to expose more skin (apparently I wasn't naked enough) and felt what could only be described as a giant cat tongue licking my entire backside. She had a loofah and was wiping it from my neck to my heels again and again. Out of my peripheral vision, I could see something gray flying all around me, and it wasn't until she whipped me over that I saw it was all my dead skin. Those poor women had to witness some first-timer getting thirty years of dead skin scrubbed off, but I'll tell you what, I was smooth as a baby's bum.

While I lay there with my arms above my head and the scrubber woman's bosoms knocking past my face as she continued to scrub me raw, I couldn't help but feel like she was angry and taking out all her aggression on me. She had a fierceness in her eyes that made her look determined to clean the foreign right off me. Peering through the steam, I looked over and saw Mia nestled between some half-clothed *teyze*s (aunties). I could see her eyes half-rolled into the back of her head and a small smile on her face. She had metaphorically shed her dead skin and was finally comfortable in her own body in front of everyone else. Although she appeared to be under the influence of something, she looked so happy and peaceful. "This is amazing," she mouthed at me while we both looked around at the beauty of the situation and what we hadn't been able to see before because of our own media-induced insecurities. Women talking and enjoying each other while bathing each other. No one was staring at the size of anyone's body parts; no one was comparing cellulite or stretch marks.

After I was done with the Cat-Lick Table, I went and sat next to Mia and together we watched a group of women that appeared to be four generations of a family. One woman must have been in her eighties; years of hard work, motherhood, and life experiences showed on every inch of her body. Her back was turned to either her daughter or daughter-in-law. The daughter (in her fifties or sixties) was washing the long grey hair of the older woman and scrubbing her back with a hand-loofah. In front of the older woman was a woman in her thirties whose skin was jaundiced and her bones were barely covered with skin. Her head was bald and it was easy to assume that she either had cancer or was recovering. She was crouched, hugging her knees, while the eighty-year-old grandmother washed her bald head softly. A little naked toddler was waddling around mom, grandma, and great-grandma, playing with a bucket of water and pouring it on each one of the women.

People often say they can feel so much love for a person or an animal or even a place, but what about a scene? I felt so much love watching this scene of four generations in the nude bathing each other. It was so symbolic and touched my core. Mia and I came out of there different people and not just because our skin was so raw it was sparkling, but because we were able to experience humanity in a way that could only be done by literally stripping off every layer.

THE HAMMAM—THROUGH MIA'S EYES

I felt like we had been driving forever. It was only a couple of hours away, but my nerves were causing time to slow down. There was nothing around us except for dry, arid, rolling hills and the road ahead.

I knew nothing about Turkey except for the fact that Alicia had moved there while I was serving a church mission. After returning home, I was determined to see Alicia and three months later, I flew to Turkey.

I'd always followed my older sisters blindly, and I trust them with my life. So, when Alicia asked me if I wanted to go to a hammam for a rich Turkish experience, I said yes.

I knew nothing about hammams.

Alicia, being the gem that she is, told me a little bit about the culture and what the crap a hammam even is. Here is what I knew:

- A hammam is a bathhouse. (I imagined dark and steamy, so dark no one could really see anything.)

- I would be wearing a bikini (which I have never worn in my life), or nothing at all.

- The end.

Alicia had a friend, Yeliz, who was from a small town (village?) in the middle of the Turkish desert. Yeliz would be our bathhouse guide and lead us to our fate. We finally pulled up to a small, modest building. Yeliz did all the talking to the person at the front desk while I tried to focus on my breathing and uncontrollable shaking. We walked back to the women's locker room, which was pointless. Who needs a changing/locker room when you're just going to strip in front of everyone anyway? Might as well get it over with and just do it in the lobby. This felt really drawn out.

According to my insecure and mortified memory, everyone was staring and whispering as they walked by, commenting on my nationality and hair color. (How would I even know what they were saying? I don't speak Turkish.) I did stick out. I was blonde. And had fair skin. At least Alicia could blend in with her dark hair and olive skin.

I truly don't remember how we got from the locker room to the bathing room. I felt like I was floating across the floor propelled by curiosity and dread. Everything was a blur...until...shock. Huge boobs, medium boobs, small boobs....You get where I'm going with this.

After some time, I came out of my terror coma and realized (I don't know how I got there or what I did before I got there) I was in a scalding pool with a rotten-egg-smelling-fountain continuously flowing into it. The ceiling let in a natural perfect light that lit up the white marble room and perfectly illuminated everything. *Everything.*

There were two open rooms separated by a natural shower pouring from the ceiling. The pool room, which I was currently in, was for soaking and preparing your skin for cleaning. The second was a square-shaped room lined with a marble bench and several basins overflowing with water. Directly in the center of the room was a large marble table and one woman designated as the washer, scrubber, terrorizer, etc.

Just as I was getting used to swimming around the pool with my top off (no one had ever seen me topless in my life—ahem, Mom), Yeliz told me it was my turn to be scrubbed. Again, I honestly do not remember how I got from the pool to the table, but there I was in the dead center of the room. Laying spread eagle on my back and my chest pointing heavenward. This. Was. Happening.

You know how when people are going under the knife, the last distinct thing they remember seeing is the bright light above their head? That was me. The bright skylights were shining directly into my eyes, yet I was awake for the entire thing. I was being soaped up very generously and before I knew it, my arms were being scrubbed raw, then my legs, stomach, and bum.

As you know, marble and soap are not the best combination for traction. I felt like a slippery fish being filleted. After she had finished my left side, the woman grabbed my bikini bottoms and WHIPPED me 180 degrees. If you've ever gotten a massage, then you're familiar with their soothing voices and slow rhythmic actions. They tell you calmly to slowly turn over to your other side. I don't think this woman had ever gotten a massage. There was nothing calming or soothing about the way she rotated me.

She proceeded to use her sandpaper (or whatever it was that she was using) to cheese-shred the perfect tan right off my body. She then mentioned something in Turkish, and Yeliz laughed. I asked Yeliz what she said and was told that the woman announced to the whole room that I "was so dirty." My turn was over and I jumped off the marble table over to the spectator benches.

I'm pretty sure she scrubbed the nerves off of me too, because once I was at the bench I could relax, I realized there were hardly any spectators. If they were watching, no one was scrutinizing bodies or comparing. I'd almost forgotten I was topless. I sat there while Alicia used the basin water to wash all of the dead skin off of me and watched the other women around the room. No one was looking at each other, or their own bodies. They were simply bathing.

To my left was a woman with a different body type than mine, lying on her side propped up with one elbow—completely exposed. She wasn't trying to cover anything.

My Westernized brain-washed mind led me to believe that only women with perfect bodies could be comfortable in their own skin. How wrong I was! Who's to say what's "perfect" and what's not? To me, SHE was perfect. She was perfect because she felt no need to hide anything and was proud of who she was. Isn't that perfect?

THE FALL

urkey, October, month sixteen

T If I could choose to erase one memory from my mind, it would probably be the one of seeing my little girl's face while falling and reaching out to us with a look of complete terror. Ironically, that will probably be the one memory I'll never be able to forget.

Saturday we went to our favorite local bakery shop that we've been coming to at least one to two times a week since we arrived. The bakery sits on a busy street lined with shops, restaurants, and bakeries connected like stalls or row houses—each one not more than ten feet wide. To accommodate customers, most of these businesses have roof access converted into a makeshift terrace for extra seating. Imagine row houses made from cement with nailed boards and plastic tarps everywhere. While the structure appears decrepit, the food is incredibly delicious and fresh. Without fail, there is a line and if you're not there early enough, you'll miss out on the best pastries or the *teyze* who stands out front in the morning juicing fresh oranges and carrots.

The cashier stands in front of a large glass case which displays every Turkish pastry you can imagine: *Gözleme, poğaça, börek, etc.* The best part is that you can buy Turkish breakfast, *köy kahvaltısı*—my absolute favorite—all day long. The second-best part is you can buy enough food to fill an entire table and it will cost no more than twelve dollars.

Having succumbed to the bakery smells wafting up our street, we went on Saturday afternoon for some *pide* and *gözleme*. Upon arrival all the lower-level tables were full, so we made our way up the extremely steep, narrow, rail-less stairs to the terrace seating. The roof is lined with a thin metal railing around the perimeter that allows Will and Ayla to run around and play without being near the street. Because our normal seats—near the giant tree that sprouted through the sidewalk below and towers over the building—were occupied, we sat at a different table near the fence separating our terrace from the roof of the next-door pizza shop. Will and Ayla were playing and jumping around while Aaron and I were just sitting there watching them and talking to each other.

While we were watching Ayla waddle around, she walked over to the fence babbling incoherently near our table and all of a sudden tripped on the little ledge that supported the fence. The next thing I know, she was gone. One second she was there and the next second she wasn't. In that split second of tripping, she put her hands out to catch her fall and rolled backward into an unseen gap, falling with the most panic-stricken look on her face, reaching up to me. Even though I watched her fall, I couldn't see the small gap between the two buildings until I jumped up. There it was, this cruel optical illusion becoming clearer and revealing this tiny gap between the ledge and the railing.

I started screaming and immediately turned to run downstairs thinking she had fallen onto the floorboards between the two levels. My first thought was that she had landed on her back and/or her head and she surely would have brain damage or be paralyzed. In a split second, I pictured a future of having to care for her for the rest of her life. I raced down the stairs, causing such a commotion that everyone stopped and looked at me, the *yabancı,* or foreigner, who was screaming incoherently and flailing her arms.

I was searching ceiling floorboards above me for any sign of her but didn't see her. All of a sudden I could hear her screaming and a sob escaped my mouth. I was so grateful that she was screaming and not silent, but when I couldn't see her, I started to run back upstairs (with a group of spectators trailing after me). I got to the bottom of the stairs and saw Aaron flying down the steps, three at a time. After seeing her fall and watching me run down the stairs, Aaron went straight to the hole, bending over it to see if he could see Ayla. He couldn't see her, but he could see that there weren't any floorboards and he could hear her screaming. We ran back to the front of the bakery near the street, searching frantically for her and desperately trying to follow her screams. The owner of the restaurant, who had been throwing chairs and tables out of the way, reached up and grabbed a huge vinyl poster that was hanging on the wall and tore it to the side, revealing a tiny gap in between the two buildings. There on the ground amid the wires and nails and debris was our Ayla on her hands and knees screaming hysterically. I ran to her and picked her up looking for any signs of blood and looking up at the little gap she had fallen through from above.

The gap was an unfinished, cinder block space between the two buildings. Up on the roof, the ground had looked flush against the ledge and railing, but in fact, there was a gap. The height from the roof terrace to the ground was around twelve to fifteen feet and no bigger than twenty-four inches wide. It was full of hundreds of wires, old stacked buckets, and leftover cinder blocks. The ground was covered with tools and nails and she had somehow landed on her hands and knees, after falling backward, in the only clear spot. I say "somehow" lightly because there is no logical explanation for her surviving after we saw all the things she could have, or should have, hit. "Somehow" means it was not her time to go and she was protected by unseen forces.

Trembling, I ran to her and hesitated for a split second, before scooping her up carefully so I wouldn't cause more damage. At that moment, I remembered Will, whom we had just left on the terrace, and heard him crying behind me. I turned to see him in the arms of a Turkish couple who were trying to calm him nearby until we finished with Ayla.

Miraculously, among the other customers who had been trailing us were some doctors who offered to look at Ayla. They cleared a table under a light just like they did in the movies by sweeping everything off in one swoop. Ayla, who was still terrified, was screaming hysterically at every touch. Oddly, she didn't have one spot of blood or a single mark on her. Not one scratch. I was so confused and shocked by everything that had happened so fast that I just went into fight or flight mode. The doctors, who were just as confused as we were when they saw where she had fallen and landed, suggested we go to the hospital to check for internal bleeding or fractures. They hadn't been able to feel any broken bones, but that didn't mean there weren't any fractures.

In a split second, I handed Ayla to Aaron and grabbed our keys and ran home as fast as I could to grab our car. Driving for the first and only time like a native Turk, I came to a screeching halt in front of the restaurant. We loaded Will in the car and Aaron held Ayla on his lap while I drove like a bat out of hell to the hospital. Together, we prayed our little hearts out and Aaron told me that when he saw her fall he thought, "I just watched my baby girl die right in front of my eyes."

By the time we got to the hospital, Ayla had calmed down and we ran into the emergency room with both kids and practically yelled that Ayla had fallen from four meters and we needed x-rays. The nurse at the desk cocked her head to the side and looked from us to Ayla, who was smiling and trying to wiggle out of Aaron's arms. I'm sure she thought we were just confused *yabancılar*, foreigners, that couldn't speak Turkish well and asked again, "How far did she fall?"

After a series of x-rays and CT scans that showed NOTHING, they sent us to another hospital for a follow-up and an MRI. By the time we got to the next hospital, Ayla and Will were chasing each other, giggling, in the lobby while Aaron and I were still frantic, unable to comprehend the lack of symptoms of such a fall. The MRI also showed nothing, and we finally accepted the fact that it really, truly was a miracle. Ayla fell from twelve to fifteen feet and landed amid debris on the cement floor and didn't even have a scratch or a bruise to show for it.

I haven't been able to go back to the restaurant yet and I don't know that I will be able to for a while, but I'm extremely grateful for the unseen angels that surely were with Ayla that day.

THE ROYALS—PART III

T*urkey, December, month eighteen*
"You are so ugly!" was said to my toddler today. Don't worry, Mama Bear didn't come out. She smiled and agreed because she has learned that this is a compliment in Turkey.

I have completely, fully, and unequivocally embraced the royal treatment of children. I think it is the most endearing cultural trait, but also one of the funniest, and it is ingrained from childhood in every Turk. The other day, we were at the park with Ayla, who is now about sixteen months, and there was a little boy about three years old playing as well. He saw Ayla walk up and he started beaming and came straight towards her to say, "I could just eat you! You're so yummy!" and then offered to help her up the ladder and down the slide. His mother then proceeded to pinch Ayla's cheeks and said, "You're so ugly! You're so ugly!!" I smiled knowing this is similar to the English phrase, "You're so stinkin' cute!"

However, some Turks take it a step further—and then a step past that. After saying, "I could just eat you!" They will follow it up with, "And I'll just add some ketchup and salt and take a little bite!" while pretending to nibble on the leg or arm. I've embraced this cultural aspect and have even come to expect it; on the rare occasion that it's not displayed around my kids, I have thought, *They must not be Turkish.* Last week's experience really takes the cake though. Just when I think I couldn't be surprised by this cultural trait anymore, I get my socks knocked off.

We went to Aaron's office to visit his colleagues and pick him up from work. He works with quite a few Turkish people and as soon as my kids entered the hallway yelling for daddy, five—FIVE—people came out of different offices to see them. It was like putting honey on the counter for ants. After my kids had been passed around, kissed on, and sugared up, I could smell that Ayla had a poopy diaper. I picked up Ayla and told Aaron that we better be going so we can change her diaper. All of a sudden, I kid you not, one of the women made a beeline to us and smashed her face right in Ayla's bum and took a big exaggerated sniff. After pulling her face out of Ayla's bum, she acted deliriously happy as if she had just been drugged and said, "Mmmmm, I could just eat your poop!"

Wowwwww. I did *not* see that one coming.

THE STARING

Turkey, February, month twenty

Do you want to know what I can't get used to? The staring. Staring is not considered rude here and I am *not* going to miss that little cultural trait. It started when I arrived so large and pregnant. I mean, I get that. I would be staring too if I saw a belly like that. After the birth, I attributed the staring to our "foreign-ness." Then it just never stopped and it started to bother me. The first few times this happened in public with someone, I just stared back and we entered into a staring contest until I caved and my foreign self had to look away. It's just a cultural difference, but it's so hard for me to change my way of thinking.

A couple of months ago we had to take Ayla to the ER because she fell off her changing table. Mother of the Year Award right here. After she fell, she wouldn't stop screaming. Fearing a fracture or concussion, we rushed her into the ER. Again. We are on a first-name basis now and practically family with the hospital staff. They quickly moved us to a sectioned-off room, but left the door open so the doctors and nurses could go in and out. After all the doctors and nurses left, we became preoccupied with calming Ayla down. After a while, I looked up to find at least four random people standing in the doorway of our room watching. I literally laughed out loud. In the States we would be curious but turn away to give others privacy. We sneak looks, but pretend we aren't looking. That's a capital NOPE here. No such thing. They just stood there watching from about eight feet away. Even when we all made eye contact and I tried to shield Ayla from their prying eyes, they just kept standing there. I wondered why they even have walls or room dividers? I probably should have just launched into what had happened and given them all of Ayla's vitals and stats, but no, I am the one who grew uncomfortable and looked away.

THE LOVELY EMPLOYMENT

Turkey, April, month twenty-two

We only have a few months left and we are getting our last stream of visitors. One of my closest friends came to visit and we took the kids and traveled north to stay in an old Ottoman house. One evening the toilet broke and I ran down to the reception desk and explained what had happened. I also asked if they could also deliver an extra blanket. After I was finished, it hit me that I had just explained a plumbing problem and asked for something *all in Turkish*. Had someone told me two years ago that I would be having this conversation in Turkish, I would have snorted. I stood there smiling and silently patted myself on the back.

A couple weeks later, still on a high from my newly realized triumph, we were watching some family videos with the kids. In one of the videos we were at Yeliz's house visiting and two little boys were dancing to the Gangnam song. I had been filming them and encouraging them by yelling, "Good job!!! Good job!" in Turkish. While we were watching it, Aaron turned to me and said, "Baaabe, what are you yelling in the background?"

"I'm telling them, '*Güzel iş!*' You know, like, 'Good job!'"

Aaron just looked at me sadly, like someone about ready to take a sucker from a child's mouth, and said, "You know that's not what it means, don't you?"

WHAT. "Well, what *do* they say then?" I said defiantly, irritated that he was questioning my Turkish abilities.

"They say *'aferin*,' which is like 'well done.' You literally just said, "Lovely employment!"

I was so embarrassed. I couldn't even listen to myself anymore and we watched the rest on mute. Why didn't the other six adults there correct me?

A couple days passed and I was on my way to lunch when I jumped in a taxi on our street. We know all the taxi drivers here really well and love them to pieces. One of the usual ones picked me up and I asked him in Turkish how everything was going. He responded with, "*Berbat!*" and threw his arms up and laughed. This was not one of the usual responses I'm aware of, so when I'm in this situation I just resort to reading facial expressions and body language. I assumed that throwing up one's arms and laughing was a good sign, so in return I threw my arms up and in Turkish I responded with "That's great! So so great. I'm so happy." Later I wanted to add it to my list of words I've learned, so I looked up *berbat* in the dictionary. Lo and behold it says, "*Awful. Wretched. Terrible. Crappy. Miserable.*"

Stupid girl. Moral of the story, don't get on your high horse, or he will kick you right off.

THE LIST

*T*urkey, *May, month twenty-three*

I have a lump in my throat. Not the Adam's Apple kind, but the kind you get when you're getting ready to say goodbye and it's going to be *really* hard. Turkey has my whole heart. Don't get me wrong, I am excited to be back in the States, but I am going to have a really hard time leaving Turkey. When I first got here I thought this was going to be the longest two years of my life. After a meltdown driven by sleep deprivation and postpartum hormones, Aaron suggested I start making lists of everything I liked about Turkey and our time here. I started looking for things every day to add to my list and it grew until I fell madly in love with Turkey. Now that I've fallen in love with it, I am having a really hard time thinking about leaving. So I've taken the same concept and applied it to the States so hopefully it won't be as hard to leave. Here are some of things I'm really looking forward to:

- Omelettes. The real ones. Not the Turkish ones. There should be a warning sign at all points of entry into Turkey for foreigners that says, "WARNING: An omelette is not an *omelette* here. At least not the kind you're expecting." The Turks make a Veggie Omelette in literal terms. I ordered an omelette once and when it arrived—well, it was not what I expected. What I expected were eggs, mushrooms, cheese, maybe some peppers and tomatoes. What I received were eggs, broccoli, cauliflower, carrots, and peas. I mean to their credit it *was* a veggie omelette...just not the veggies I am used to.

• Parking lots. They don't exist in the city. People just put on their hazards and stop in the middle of the road because there's nowhere to park. No exaggeration. The one time I found the only parking "garage" I've ever seen, I pulled down this extremely steep ramp just to come to a dead end. There was a wall in front of me and a wall on either side of me. I started panicking about reversing back up the steep slope when I saw a man come out of nowhere waving his arms and telling me to stop. He then proceeded to crank something and my entire car turned around on a turntable. A giant, metal Lazy Susan. All of a sudden I was faced backward and could see another giant slope under the first one down to a garage that I couldn't see before. Genius, I tell you! And scary as ever. Sweaty armpits for sure.

• Squirrels. I miss the little rats. They are everywhere in the States, but I haven't seen one here except in the zoo (where they have an entire enclosure just for squirrels). Now I understand why I have seen so many Asian tourists taking pictures of squirrels.

• Zoos. A real zoo. The one here is hilarious and sad all at the same time. I don't know what I was expecting, but it was not seeing cages full of domesticated house pets like Beagles and Golden Retrievers next to the cats and pigeons.

• Drive-thrus! I haven't seen a drive-thru in two years! I'm not kidding, the business would boom for these restaurants and coffee shops if they just installed a drive-thru. Especially because there's nowhere to park anyway.

• Ending this two-year game of charades. I have probably reached expert level by now, but I'm ready to tap out for sure.

Yeah, I'm still working on the rest of the list. It's not very long, which just says that I will miss Turkey more than I ever imagined possible.

THE DEPARTURE—TURKEY

USA, July, month twenty-five

It's no secret that moving to Turkey was quite a shock to my system, but now I'm having a hard time accepting that our time is done and I'm back Stateside.

The day we left, the entire neighborhood came out to say goodbye. Mustafa, the street valet; all the taxi drivers; the two restaurant owners; the security guards (who made a CD of Turkish music for Ayla so she could remember her birth country); our building manager; the bank security guard; and of course Belgin and Bilge. Belgin told us to knock on her door when we were getting in the taxi and she would walk out with us. When we knocked on her door she answered it dressed in her housecoat, no bra, Chanel slippers, and holding a bucket of water.

Belgin proceeded to follow us downstairs with her bucket of water (which I assumed from the way she was dressed was dirty mop water she was coming to throw outside). After tears and hugs and kisses, we got in the taxi and started to drive away. At that point, Belgin took the bucket of water and threw it behind the taxi. I have no idea what it was for, but it was a cultural thing and I knew it was meant to be a good thing. From the back of the taxi, I watched everyone waving goodbye until we were out of sight and I realized that I left a piece of my heart there for good.

PART II - BELGIUM

I think I'm quite ready for another adventure.
-Bilbo Baggins

THE MEANTIME

Remember how I said I wanted to have another baby in Turkey? We almost extended our time there. Two weeks before we left, Aaron was asked if we wanted to extend another year. Had we been asked that question the year before, I would have said yes on the spot. However, two weeks before departing, I was already in the mindset of being back in the States and so we declined and came home. I'm glad we did, because Baby Number Three came to this world on a wild ride shortly after, and had we been in another country, I don't know if either of us would have survived. I thought for sure we would be Stateside for at least five years, but we were soon itching to be overseas again. When Baby Number Three, named Gracie, was about two years old, we saw a position open in Belgium and applied. In September, Aaron received news that he got the job and he would leave in February. We decided that he would go and we would join him in June when school was finished for the year. Apparently, we are all more dependent on each other than we realized, because we made it about eight weeks before saying, "Forget this. We need each other." We packed up to join Aaron in Belgium.

THE FIRST WEEK

B*elgium, May, month one*
We'reeeee here!!! Bloodshot eyes and all. Jet lag is a real beast and I'm sure I was slurring my words to whomever I spoke to that first day. I don't even remember. Aaron arrived two months ago while I packed up and he looked for a house. After weeks of searching, he finally found a house way out in the countryside on the French-Belgian border. It's about thirty minutes to his work, but we decided that since the kids are going to a local school instead of the international one in the bigger city, it's OK to commute. We are here for the next three years and we thought it would be a good opportunity for the kids to learn French. But to really do that, we've chosen to completely immerse ourselves—i.e. move far away from anything that might be comfortable. Ummm, yeah. I'm still laughing at my naive little self.

Today we went to church for the first time. There is an English-language congregation near Aaron's work but again, why do things easy when you can do them HARD? Ugggh. Actually, jokes aside, we felt strongly that we should attend services with the French language congregation, just across the border in France. I was really nervous for the kids at first, but they just went with the flow. A sweet older Chilean-French woman sat next to me and because at this point I know more words in Spanish than French (but still knew minimal Spanish), she insisted on translating for me. I was laughing to myself thinking, *I'm sitting in a small town in France and my brain physically hurts because I'm trying to understand French and now it's at migraine status because I'm trying to understand Spanish too.* I loved her so much though and was so appreciative that she was trying to help me. (Brain aches from concentrating is a real thing. I'm not kidding. Don't google it, just trust me).

There is a sweet seventeen-year-old Belgian girl with Down's Syndrome who made me feel the most welcome. From my short time here, I've already learned that while the francophones of southern Belgium and Northern France are cordial and polite, they are not known to be loud, warm, or overly friendly people. They don't want to intrude on your personal space. I say all this so you understand how much I appreciated and needed this sweet girl. Through the *entire* service she was turning around and winking at me while blowing kisses. She followed that by making the heart shape with her hands and then pointing to me and then making the heart shape again. She and two-year-old Gracie had an impromptu sing-off to see who could sing the hymns loudest. It was hilarious because neither one of them knew the words and so it was more a battle of the sounds. In a 20x20 square foot room with tile floors.

Speaking of Gracie, she has been the funniest to watch adjusting to this new life. She recognizes that everyone is not speaking English, so when they talk to her, she just responds with "Blah blah blah." (Literally—"blah blah.") She makes us laugh. She is quickly realizing that in order to communicate with people, she needs to say these new sounds she hears. The other night it was her turn to pray and it went something like this, "Dear Heavenly Father, goo ga ga. Coo coo feya *enchante*. Gee gee *toilette* goo gee. Lu lu...uh...mix it, pat it, and throw it in the air!"

In other Cardway news, Will and Ayla have had the best time laughing at the statue of a naked lady at the entrance of our little neighborhood. The statue sits in a fork in the road and you can go either right or left. They have figured out that we have to follow the "right boob" to get to our house. When I give them a stern look for laughing about it, they just say, "What?! She's the one who's naked!"

We can't wait for everyone to visit! Just follow the ~~yellow brick road~~ naked lady statue.

THE JOB

Belgium, May, month one

B We've been here a little over a week, and I got a job! Kind of. I think? It was all in French, so it's hard to tell. Remember the extent of my French is twenty words—I know, right? I'm practically fluent.

But first...the kids started school this week. Are we horrible parents? They're not even over jet lag. Four days after our arrival we said, "School starts tomorrow!" We were trying to keep them in a routine and make the transition as easy as possible. Why not add a new school to the mix of new home, new country, and new language? Don't judge. There are no instruction manuals for how to raise kids overseas.

I have had so much anxiety about putting them in a local Belgian school, but we felt like it is a great, unique opportunity. I was mostly worried about Will, who is seven years old, almost eight. I worried he would hate it and want to quit immediately. The girls had been interested in French for months before our arrival, but Will showed no interest. He kept saying, "I will learn it when I get there."

We got to school and Will and Ayla were instant celebrities. We live in a small village out in the countryside and I doubt many locals have ever met an American. Everyone loved them and when I picked them up (for three days in a row now), they both came out jumping and squealing, "This is the best day EVER!" In the courtyard, five to six kids are constantly swarming Will at any given time. Yesterday he yelled at me from afar and said, "Mom! How do I say, 'I need space' in French?!"

Gracie, on the other hand, is a hot mess. She is almost three years old and went from being home with me all day to a new country, language, and full-time school. The second day was awful. I felt like I was failing my child by putting her in that situation. Tears were shed, on her part too, and I tried to talk to the principal, but when I only know twenty words that consist of "hello," "goodbye," "thank you," "yellow," "red," "apple," etc., it's kind of hard. She called a friend who speaks English, because Aaron, who speaks French too, was unavailable to translate for me. I tried to ask if the school wanted me to stay or go and what would be best in this situation, and the person relayed that it was best for me to just leave. I mustered up the courage to go and the principal walked me downstairs...straight into Gracie's classroom and handed Gracie to me. Uhhhhh, what? Was she letting me say goodbye? Was she telling me to stay with her? Or was she telling me to take Gracie home?

So, I stayed. *Duh.*

Later, after getting home from school, I emailed the principal (with my trusty Google Translate) and said that I could stay any time they thought necessary and explained that parents often volunteer in schools in America. She responded and Google Translate told me she said, "Wonderful. The teacher would be very happy."

As I walked in today with Gracie, promising her I would stay, the teacher told me (I think) that she was indeed so happy to have an assistant. I ended up staying the whole day again and when I left she said cheerfully, "See you tomorrow!" (Which I had to look up because I didn't know what it meant). Was that a "See you tomorrow when you drop Gracie off" or was that a "See you tomorrow as my assistant"?

SO, the question is, am I her assistant or not? Will I be the weird American mom that just, "bless her heart," shows up everyday thinking she has a responsibility? Or will I be the weird American mom that said she would help at the school and didn't follow through?

This is so stressful.

The school

THE UNJOB

Belgium, May, month one
Ummm, my job as an assistant at the kids' school turned out NOT to be a job, but more of a "Bless her heart—how do we get rid of the foreign lady?" How awkward is that? So awkward, I tell you. Cringe-worthy awkward. When you don't speak a language, you get *really* good at reading expressions and cues. It's like developing a sixth sense. Based on little looks and nods in my direction, I started to get that funny little feeling that I wasn't supposed to be the teacher's assistant .

Want to know what it feels like? Just walk into any establishment and pretend you were hired. Go ahead, try it. Just walk right in and sit down with a big ol' goofy grin and start speaking in a language they don't understand.

I should have known they wouldn't hire a preschool teacher who can't. even. speak. to. the. kids. I used a lot of "Wowwww! Cool!" and "*Très bien*!" with a French accent, of course. Well, one of the days, this little boy came up to me pointing and telling me excitedly about what I thought was a project he was working on and so I said, "*Ohhh! Très bien, Pierre*!!!" Turns out he was telling me that another little boy hit him and took his toy. No wonder they didn't want me there.

Now I'm back at home nursing my pride, knowing that I will have to face these teachers every single day for the next three years.

THE DEATH TRAP

B *elgium, May, month one*

Although we had just arrived in Belgium and were still dealing with jet lag, we took the kids to Paris for the weekend to stay with and visit friends we'd met while living in Turkey. It's a quick two-and-a-half-hour drive, so what better way to get over jet lag?

Aaron and I had been to Paris before, but this was our kids' very first time. Wanting to check off our list of must-sees, we first headed to the Arc de Triomphe. The Arc is a monument that was constructed to commemorate Napoléon I's victory at the Battle of Austerlitz in 1805 and if you can make it up all 164 feet, or 348 stairs, it is the best spot to view all of Paris with the view of the Eiffel Tower in the background. It's considered a main attraction in Paris, along with the Eiffel Tower and Notre Dame, sitting at the end of the famous Avenue des Champs Elysees. (Pronounced *Shonz Elle Ease Say.* Future-me is now saying, "You're welcome" to future-you for preventing you from making the same mistake I made.)

If you haven't been there, the Arc de Triomphe is in the middle of a HUGE roundabout—we're talking approximately eight lanes of traffic circling the monument. Just as we had done on our anniversary trip (without the kids), Aaron and I got ready to ninja-move across all eight lanes to make it to the Arc. Lining the streets facing the roundabout are hundreds of tourists taking pictures and gawking at the beauty of Napoléon's triumph. We pushed our way up to the curb, proudly displaying that we weren't afraid to cross the lanes that we assumed were stopping all of them from doing the same. Aaron picked up our two younger girls, one in each arm, and I grabbed Will's hand. I felt like we were taking part in the running of the bulls. We waited an eternity for a small break and ran two lanes, immediately stopping before getting bug-squashed. We waited a little more and ran two to three more lanes before stopping again. We were literally dodging and zig-zagging.

Do you know the scene from *Ocean's Twelve* when the acrobat guy had to crawl through all the security laser beams to steal something? Yeah, we looked just like that, except on fast forward because the cars were *not* slowing down and apparently Parisian drivers don't care much for jaywalking tourists. I kept looking across and seeing all the tourists at the Arc already and was thinking, *How on earth did they not die? How have there not been more accidents here? This is a death trap!*

We made it across and caught our breath while slightly bent over with our hands on our knees. I swear our children's eyes were wide and bloodshot, having narrowly avoided becoming roadkill. We casually gave a thumbs-up to other nearby tourists who must have made it across as well.

It was then that out of the corner of our eyes, we saw swarms of people ascending from underground. While we stood there with our heads cocked to the side and mouths wide open, we saw the stairs that led down to a tunnel that allows tourists to safely cross. We slowly turned to face each other.

Fools. We had just become *those* tourists.

Embarrassed and laughing, we quickly grabbed the kids' hands and headed away from anyone that had just witnessed the idiots cross eight lanes of traffic with three small children under the age of seven.

"Well-traveled parents" for the win.

THE BISE

B elgium, May, month one
Welcome to *La Bise* culture. (Pronounced "beez.") The *bise,*
or *bisous*, are about as awkward for Americans as hugging is for
Europeans. Everyone knows kissing is a way of greeting here. I pride
myself on *not* being the awkward foreigner that can't adjust to local
customs and norms. Turns out I AM the awkward foreigner. There
should be a *Bise 101* class for all incoming native English speakers
trying to assimilate. We live right on the border of Belgium and France
and apparently in northern France they kiss both cheeks and in
Belgium they kiss one. Well, this useful tidbit of information was not
in my Welcome Packet upon arrival. I didn't know this and my first
exposure to the kiss greetings was at church—in France—with the
double kisses.

Back at home—in Belgium—I saw my next-door neighbor and he
came to greet me with a kiss and I—trying to prove I'm the "assimilated
un-awkward foreigner"—did the same. Exxxxcept he stopped after one
bisou and stepped back while I proceeded to lean to the other side and
kiss the air.

You can't cover that up.

THE HARD THINGS

B *elgium, June, month two*
Last week a lot of tears were shed and prayers were said. Navigating a new country and language, in particular with children in tow, is hard. When we arrived, our family came up with a new motto: Cardways Do Hard Things. We knew it would be hard, but I wasn't prepared for *how* hard it would be—especially doing it the way we've done it. Let me just say that I love living here and I love all the awesome opportunities it offers. Still, not even cobblestone streets and *pain au chocolat* can cure this mama's broken heart.

The kids' school is in the center of the village and all the parents park their cars on the surrounding streets and walk their kids to the courtyard. After dropping the kids off, I went back to my car and saw that I had a perfect view of the courtyard. I sat there for a while watching and noticed Will walking around alone on the playground. The novelty of a new foreign student has worn off and now Will is just, well, foreign. I've been there. I know that feeling of being at a new school and not having friends yet. I watched Will get out a little notepad from his backpack—the same notepad he and Aaron worked on for an hour the night before. Will had come home asking how to say certain things and then wrote them down phonetically on a notepad. I watched Will pull out this same notepad and walk up to some boys and read some of his phrases. I could see the confused look on their faces and then I could see Will either read it again or try a different phrase. I sat there watching him, forbidding myself to go running to his rescue as the boys snickered and walked away exchanging glances.

I watched Will stand there for a minute and then try it again with someone else only to have the same thing happen. I'm fully aware that things could be so much worse, but watching your child suffer in any way is excruciating. I could still see my two-year-old Will running into my room and saluting me while yelling, "I'n a soldier, Mommy, I'n a tough soldier."

He finally sat down by himself against the wall until the bell rang. I watched as all other students formed a line to enter the school and saw Will finally stand up and trail a few feet behind the last kid in line. This is what he had meant when he had been telling me all week that he's so lonely. I sat there for another fifteen minutes sobbing alone in my car. Through the snot and tear wiping, I pleaded with God to let us know if we had made a mistake. Aaron and I had really felt good about this area, but now I questioned everything.

I opened my scripture app on my phone, hoping to get some divine inspiration. God didn't make me wait long this time and He answered my prayers immediately. The very FIRST scripture passage I came across while sitting there basically said, "I've sent you to this area. Be faithful in tribulation, for after much tribulation come the blessings." Right. To. Me. I sniffled, started the car, and drove home.

God didn't immediately take away the broken heart, but I did feel encouraged and lifted. The next day, after more tears (my tears) were shed at drop-off, I opened the same app to listen to some sermons while doing dishes. As I was searching for one, the year 1996 randomly popped into my head and then was followed immediately by the month of April. I scrolled until I found April 1996 and scrolled through the titles of sermons for that month. Low and behold there was one titled "Facing Trials with Optimism" from April 1996. (No, I'm not kidding.) I don't believe in coincidences, but I do believe He is aware of each and every one of us, from serious trials to a mama's little broken heart in a tiny village in Belgium.

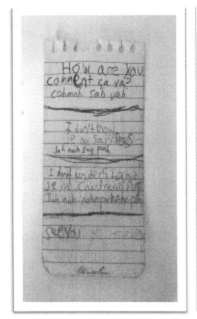

Eight-year-old Will's notepad pages

THE FRENCHEMIES

Belgium, June, month two

After recent experiences, I decided to really buckle down on my French learning. If my children are going to learn it, then I am too so I can help them. This is what my days consist of now: French class. French workbooks. French conversations. French headaches.

The French language and I fight. A lot. We are like Frenemies. (Or Frenchemies—see what I did there??) Our relationship typically consists of French keeping me at arm's length and me trying my hardest to make French like me.

I came to Belgium with such a positive attitude about "us all learning French!" (said in my most annoying cheerful voice), and French has knocked me down again and again. For some reason (that reason being my kids), I keep getting back up. Remember our motto is "Cardways Do Hard Things," so how can I not keep going?

Most days (around 90 percent of the time) I laugh about it. Some days I bawl my eyes out and want to give up. And then some days I have the most beautiful conversation with someone in French and think, "This isn't that hard." Like I said, Frenchemies.

I had an "ah-ha" moment yesterday. Sometimes I wish I didn't have them, because then I become retroactively embarrassed. The first couple of weeks all the kids would laugh when my kids would call out, "Mommy!" when I came to pick them up from school. Then I would get odd looks from some of the parents or grandparents when they heard my kids call out to me. I attributed this to their surprise at hearing English in a small village.

Something similar happened when we met our next-door neighbors. Early on we realized we live next door to a house for people with cognitive impairments (think brain injuries or Dementia). It's quite difficult to tell who works there and who is a resident. There is one person in particular who we truly can't figure out. Some days we think he definitely lives there and other days we think he works there. He *loves* to talk to us and asks all sorts of questions about America to which I constantly reply, "*Je ne comprends pas* (I don't understand)." One day all the kids came out to the backyard yelling, "Mommy!!" and this really confused our neighbors. One resident who speaks a little English said, "You are the mom *or* the mommy?" I replied, "Yes! Mom and mommy!" The others said something to each other in French that I didn't understand and I started to feel insecure and unsuccessfully tried to leave the conversation. Finally, when Aaron came home and I mouthed "help me," he came over and spoke to them but also ended up really confused. I asked him what they were saying and he said, "I don't really understand. I think maybe they're the ones that live there. He's asking me things that don't make sense, like, 'In America, do girls get married really, really young?'" Obviously, I was elated and flattered that they thought I looked so young. *Stop. Stop it some more!* I practically floated back to the house on my beaming pride while our neighbors walked away even more confused.

Well, a few days ago at school pick-up, I heard two little French-speaking girls call out to a much older woman, "Mommy!" and I. Was. So. Confused. Mother/mom in French is *mère/maman*. Grandmother is *grand-mère*. So why was this little girl calling her grandma "Mommy" in English? I knew I was missing something and I whipped out Google Translate for Mommy. Low and behold, it said "*Mamie,*" which means "Granny."

Oh. My. Gosh. Now I understand why my neighbors were so confused when I told them I was both the mom and the granny or why

all the kids at school don't understand why my kids call me "Granny."
Oh, bless my heart. This language is killing me.

I need to document these things so one day, months from now
when I've learned a little more, it can serve as a reminder that there is
some progress being made—especially on the days I cry from being
overwhelmed or can't turn my head because of a stress knot in my
shoulder—I call it the "French Knot." Many have asked why we are
doing this to ourselves and continuing to learn French. Believe me, I've
been the first one to ask. Every day. We are doing this for a few reasons
actually: a) The experience of living overseas completely changes when
you know the language. b) I'm in charge of the primary children in our
French-speaking church. How can I lead and teach if I don't speak their
language? c) I doubt we will leave our children with a ton of money
one day and even though they could participate in various sports or
activities (which are SO good for them), there is such a small chance
they would ever use it consistently through life. We aren't exactly the
most coordinated people, so they're kind of doomed in the sports or
dance arena. The one thing we can give them is knowledge and an extra
language and hope that it can be used to their advantage, whether that's
through school, college, career, or life in general. If they're going to
maintain it, we need to learn it too.

THE WORLD IS YOUR PLAYGROUND URINAL

B *elgium, July, month three*
Call me a prude, but I cannot believe that I have just seen three, THREE, men peeing on the side of the road within a span of a hundred yards. Don't even pretend like you wouldn't make a U-turn and go back to make sure you were seeing things correctly. When we had been given a list of cultural norms in Europe and Belgium, public peeing was not one of them.

The first guy I saw was a mail carrier. I was *bouche bée*—or open-mouth gaping—like a southern church lady watching a hussy walk into Sunday morning services. My hand flew over my mouth and my neck turned so hard it cracked. I continued driving when I saw another man on the other side of the road in business casual attire also pulled over on the side of the road, peeing next to his Mercedes. I gasped looking around like, "Do they know what will happen if the cops see them?!" After seeing a third man peeing next to a church, I flipped a U-ey and drove back around again. Yep, I was seeing things right and what was even more confusing was that they were peeing as if this were completely acceptable. It made sense now why some of the little kids at school just dropped their pants and peed in the corner of the courtyard. I attributed it to their age, but now I realized it had been a learned behavior, because it's socially acceptable.

This probably all ties into the shared bathrooms. For weeks now I've held my bladder because I couldn't find the women's restroom in various restaurants. It wasn't until going to the restroom in church that I realized there ISN'T a women's bathroom, they're all unisex bathrooms. I walked into one stall at church and our bishop walked into the stall next to mine. Nope, not awkward at all. This takes "church family" to a whole new level.

The children's bathrooms are the same at the school. Boys and girls share a bathroom with multiple stalls from kindergarten up to sixth grade. Can you imagine how much time and energy would have been saved in the US debate over the unisex bathrooms in public schools? Meanwhile, Europe is over here like, "Stoop-eed Uhmerrrrikens. Joost sink about eet."

Yesterday, I was confronted with a situation where I could have been either the awkward expat or embraced my new reality. I was probably somewhere in between the two. We were in the middle of Ghent and all three kids had to use the bathroom. I walked into a public restroom located in one of the town squares' underground parking garages. A man was washing his hands and a woman was coming out of a stall, while I was directing the two older kids to a stall. I turned and noticed a man peeing in the urinal right there not even a foot away. He looked me in the eyes and did the most culturally European polite thing to do and said, "Bonjour." I instantly felt awkward and was trying to figure out if I should have waited outside the door or if I should stay in there and act normal and just blend in. The funniest thing is that our kids weren't even fazed and just acted like, "Of course this is normal." They said, "Bonjour" back to Urinal Man and walked into separate stalls. Meanwhile, I pretended to be all of a sudden very interested in the design of the ceiling for the next five minutes.

Later, in another public restroom in town (our kids drink a lot of water), we were waiting in line and there was a group of other Americans fresh off the cruise boat. I overheard them trying to figure out where the women's bathroom was when the bathroom attendant motioned for one husband to use the freshly wiped down urinal and for the wife to take stall number two next to the urinal. Bless her tourist heart, she about had an episode. She was trying to speak "AMERICAN" to the bathroom attendant but wasn't being understood. I put on my ever-knowledgeable experienced expat hat and walked up to her explaining that it was a unisex bathroom and in places other than malls and airports, we all shared bathrooms. I acted like I'd been living here for years.

THE FAKE FRIENDS

*B*elgium, *July, month three*

We recently took a day trip to the most beautiful chateau nestled in the hills in France in the middle of nowhere. It was only an hour and a half away from our house. Driving over the hills and seeing the *Chateau de Pierrefonds* sitting majestically above the quaint little village just takes your breath away. Go ahead and look it up. It's straight out of a fairytale.

We parked and walked the streets, taking in every sound, smell, and sight. Walking towards the little village, we passed an antique shop and I about died. This was my first time going to or seeing an antique shop while living here and I LOVE OLD THINGS. I've always said that if I could have one superpower, it would be to be able to touch any object and see where it's been and who owned it. Aaron said he'd keep the kids outside while I went in and looked. I immediately started envisioning each piece in a different part of my home. When I was just about done, I saw the most beautiful, old, rustic mirror hanging on the wall. I *had* to have it. It would match perfectly with my wannabe rustic chic farmhouse style. Mind you, we have an ultra-modern house here in Belgium and a 1950s rambler back in the States, so I say "wannabe" style because really, we don't have it. I stared at it forever and saw the price tag, which was comically cheap, knowing it could go for four times that amount in the US. THEN, when I was about to purchase my little souvenir, I saw the *solde* tag hanging from it. Deflated, I walked out of the store, telling myself I'd find another one in our remaining three years in Europe.

A few weeks went by and while still thinking constantly of my Magic Mirror on the Wall, I went to the mall one day to run a few errands. When I walked into the mall I saw that every single store had giant *SOLDE* signs in their windows. Confused, I whipped out my Google Translate and saw that *solde* actually means "sale" in French. Evil, evil, mean language! My mirror was not sold; it had been on SALE. I literally calculated the time and distance to that little town to see if I could make it back before the kids were out of school, but even if I did go, there was no guarantee my mirror was still there. It will forever be "the one that got away."

There is actually a term for this sort of thing between French and English. It's called *faux amis,* or "fake friends," which is fitting because just when you think you're starting to understand someone or something, like the French language for example, it turns on you and stabs you in the back. Wa-la. Fake friends. *Faux amis* are words in French that sound exactly like words in English but have a completely different meaning. This is really confusing because there are so many words in French that are the same as in English, for example, *relation* is "relation" and *coincidence* is "coincidence." There are thousands of them, so how do I know when one of them is fake and hiding in plain sight?

Keep your friends close and your enemies closer, folks.

THE LUXEMBOURG CEMETERY

L uxembourg, July, month three

L We are about three months into our three-year tour and just did our first big road trip in Europe! We traveled for nine days, saw thirteen cities and four countries, and drove twelve hundred miles. Our last stop was in Luxembourg because we really wanted to see the American Military Cemetery there.

It didn't take me long before I was bawling, which quite disturbed our three-year-old. "What's wrong, *Maman*??!" She has taken to calling me that sometimes since she started learning French and hears all the other kids call their moms *maman*. I did not expect to be emotional at all when we pulled up to the cemetery. I am fascinated by all things World War II and was really looking forward to visiting the memorial; however, I did not think it would hit me so hard. It physically hurt my heart to think that these boys never made it home and will never be buried near family or on home soil. Through my tears, I stopped and said to my daughter, "Honey, all of these young boys were soldiers for America in a big war and died here." She looked around and threw her hands out and said, "Uhhh what boyths, Mom??" Oh yes. Obviously she couldn't see any boys. So I said, "Honey, you can't see them because they all died and now they are buried in the ground. Where all of these crosses are. Like this one. His name is Sam," I said, gesturing to a nearby headstone and reading the engraved name. She got this pitiful look on her face and almost in a whisper just said, "Tham?" in her cute little lisp. She then proceeded to stand on her tip-toes, wrap her arms around the cross, and hug the cross headstone. I cried even harder then, ob-vi-ous-ly. Then she walked to the next one and did the same. I had to stop her after a while because, well, there are 5,000 graves.

Later that night (hours later) we got home and I put her to bed and then she said, "Maman, Tham died, huh?" I was so confused. "Sam? Who's Sam? Who died?" Then it hit me and I was so touched that she was still thinking of Sam. Buried in the ground so far from home. At age nineteen.

Grant us grace fearlessly to contend against evil and to make no peace with oppression. –Prayer for Social Justice, on a plaque at the cemetery.

THE CONFRONTATION

I reland, September, month five

We just got back from Ireland and it was incredible...besides the fact that Aaron almost went viral in one of those confrontation-on-an-airplane videos. You know, the ones that the world watches and then scratches their heads about why Americans fight on airplanes so much? I'm sure if we had been in the States, everyone would have been camera ready to record the situation, but thankfully we are in Europe, where flight-fights are still a bit of an anomaly and people aren't camera ready for it.

The plane had two rows of three seats on each side. Aaron was sitting in an aisle seat with Will and Ayla next to him, and Gracie was directly across from Aaron in the aisle seat. I was in the middle and another gentleman on my left next to the window.

While Aaron was engaged with Will and Ayla, I was talking to the passenger on my left and Gracie was just watching a show on the iPad. Unbeknownst to both Aaron and me—our heads were turned in opposite directions—Gracie was bouncing her leg while watching the show and she kept kicking the chair in front of her (as three-year-olds do). Aaron and I happened to turn back towards Gracie at the exact moment the man in front of her reached behind in a rage and smacked her leg. (He might say he "swatted" and I might say he "assaulted" her, but that's beside the point. He was angry, and physical contact was made.) The upper-class, business-like Frenchman in his sixties had no idea that Aaron, across the aisle with a clear view, was her dad. He must have just imagined he could get his point across discreetly by

120

hitting her behind his chair. The poor guy had no idea what was coming to him. Let's just say that my calm, diplomatic, level-headed hubby put the fear of God in him. Aaron stood up and all of a sudden, his 6'4" frame became eight feet and he towered over the dude, growling through clenched teeth, "Did YOU just hit my daughter?! Did. You. Just. HIT. My. THREE. Year. Old. Daughter?!" I could see between the chairs that this guy had physically crouched back against his wife in the middle seat—trying to become as small as possible. From both ends of the plane, the flight attendants swiftly made their way to Aaron as fast as little buzzing bees. The Frenchman looked like one might look before getting hit by a car and quietly said, in French, "I don't speak English. I speak French." Aaron responded by snarling, "C'EST BIEN PARCE QUE JE PARLE AUSSI LE FRANÇAIS!! (THAT'S GOOD BECAUSE I ALSO SPEAK FRENCH!)." When I think back on this situation, in my memory Aaron all of a sudden has foam at the mouth and is spraying spittle on this poor man as he's growling. I was bawling because I was so angry. Why do I have to cry when I'm mad? Why can't I be like the spittle-growling husband in defense of my kids? Instead, I'm just a teary ninny.

Poor Gracie was shaking and screaming at a high pitch for the remainder of the flight. I hope the dude liked crying more than his seat being kicked. When the flight landed, Aaron stood up first to show this little man how tall he really is and practically dared him to look our daughter's way one more time. The man kept his gaze to the floor the entire time and we exited the plane on opposite ends. Wouldn't you know that of the thousands of people going through passport control and heading to one of nine different rental car companies, we had to be on the same eight-seat rental car shuttle. *Awkwardddd.* We boarded the shuttle, saw the man, and Gracie immediately started crying again. His wife just started laughing (like, "what are the odds?") while he just stared out the window the whole time.

Moral of the story, don't kick airplane seats; don't be a ninny; and don't smack a Gracie in front of her daddy.

THE NERVOUS MOTHER—PART I

B*elgium, September, month five*
School started again and after a nice long summer of traveling and relaxing, the kids must have thought the "French school" nightmare was over. Just when they thought this place might not be so bad, we threw them back into school. (I've already started saving for therapy.) Gracie has had such a hard time and cried again for the first three days. Ayla is a stereotypical middle child that just goes with the flow and is surrounded by girls constantly screaming her name, much like a typical Fan Club. Will is in pretty good spirits even though he had a recent rough interaction with an "upper-classman" (fifth grader). I'm not kidding when I say it's like *The Hunger Games* every day at recess. I constantly see kids leaving school with bloody knees, lips, or foreheads. Unless a bone is broken, the teachers don't even call home to let parents know. Fights are a common occurrence, but then those same kids will be best friends the next day. I figured that because the school is so small and everyone knows each other, they're all like siblings...except that they aren't and they get into knock-down-drag-out fights. When bringing up Will's interaction with one of the teachers, I was searching Google Translate for the word *bully*. It doesn't exist! *Harass or harassment* does, but not *bully*. This has been one of the bigger cultural changes for us. It could be a European thing or just the village where we live—I don't know, so don't quote me on it.

Today I had an appointment to obtain my Belgian ID card and when I was returning home and passing the school, I could see kids in the courtyard for recess. Obviously, I did what any mother would do and pulled over to watch them. I just wanted to check on Will, who often just walks around by himself or talks to his sisters through the gates separating the upper school from the lower school (where both his sisters are). I didn't want him to see me, so I just slipped out of the car and tiptoed to a large bush in front of the school. I was trying to look through the bush to find Will when I heard behind me, "*Madame? Ca va?* (Ma'am, you OK?)." I turned to see the *directrice* of the school standing by her Porsche in her leather jacket, stilettos, and Chanel handbag. Standing there in my T-shirt, flip-flops and NOT my Chanel handbag, I started bumbling.

It's one thing to blush and try and explain yourself in ENGLISH, but then to just stumble and try to say it in FRENCH is a different story. All that came out was, "Oh! Ha ha [*pause*] ha ha ha ha ha [*nervous giggles*]. Uhhh, je suis une maman. Je suis nerveuse! (I am a mom. I am nervous!")." (Buuuuut I'm also a creeper who is stalking my kid at the playground and I don't know how to say that in French, so...please don't arrest me.)

The side of her mouth turned slightly upward, either a smile or a twitch. She nodded ever so slightly and silently watched me make my way back to the car.

The walk of shame just took on a whole new meaning.

THE NEW FRIENDS

B*elgium, October, month six*

After many tears, our prayers were answered for Will. The novelty of being the new kid wore off quickly, and he's been so lonely at school. He goes with the "special" teacher most days to practice speaking French. One day a few weeks ago, Will came home from school and said, "Mom, what does '*nul*' mean?" I told him I didn't know, but asked how it was used. He said, "The kids at school say, '*Will est nul! Will est nul!*'" I whipped out the dictionary and saw the translation: "Will is nothing," or "Will is dumb."

I'm not lying when I say that I think I heard my heart shatter inside. It was a good opportunity to explain that kids can be cruel while not realizing what they're doing; they make fun of what they don't know or are insecure about. It was also a good opportunity to teach him to always look out for the new kid or someone else who is being made fun of because now he knows how it feels.

Aaron and I talked about it later privately and prayed he would find a friend. Any friend. A friend that didn't care if Will doesn't speak French yet. God answered quickly because two days later at the Back-to-School open house, we met Marissa. She is a very bubbly, loud, Italian-Belgian mother who was so excited to practice her elementary English. She told us that her son, Nathan, was in Will's class and she wants them to be friends because she wants Nathan to learn English. She turned from us smiling and then full-on screeeeeamed across the courtyard to her son, "NATHAN!!! NATHAN!!! Get over here RIGHT NOW!" She stopped screaming and turned back to us smiling and sweetly said, "He's coming!" Aaron and I were squeezing each other's hands so hard to keep from laughing.

Little Italian Fabio in the making came running over with his long, luscious curly dark hair flowing in the wind. His confidence was tangible and he smiled really big and said, "Hallo!"

A playdate was set up the following week and you better believe I pulled out all the stops. I had cookies, sodas, crepes, popcorn....The boys played Legos, soccer, and video games. I had "cool" music blaring and it was one disco ball short of being a house party. They couldn't speak to each other, but they had a blast.

We invited their family over the following week for dinner to help solidify the friendship. It was probably quite the cultural experience for them as well since we don't drink and didn't offer any beers. What is a dinner party without beers in Belgium? And as usual, we prayed before we ate and thought nothing of it. In typical American fashion, we ate dinner at 6 p.m. and then kicked them out after two and a half hours so we could put the littles to bed. (We had yet to learn of the European *it's-rude-if-you-leave-before-four-hours* tradition).

They left and a week later invited us over with four other families for dinner. Marissa told me they would start early because she knows our kids eat and go to bed early, and I was so humbled by her thoughtfulness. We showed up at 5:30 p.m. and were the first ones there. (We also had yet to learn of the *never-show-up-on-time-it's-rude* tradition). I hadn't fed my kids since lunch because I wanted to make sure they were good and hungry to eat all she had prepared. So when 7 p.m. rolled around and we were STILL the only ones there and my kids were waving the white flag of starvation, I asked Marissa if she had some chips or crackers or something. She ran to grab the charcuterie board she had been saving (*hiding*) and brought it out. Thinking that was dinner, my kids devoured the entire plate. The doorbell started ringing at 7:30 p.m. The families started showing up, and the beer started flowing. Since the charcuterie board was eaten, there was no food to help slow the effect of alcohol and they all quickly had a buzz.

Everyone was so nice to us and tried to include us in their conversations and talk to us, but because I had been learning French for a hot second, and their French was slurred, I had no clue what anyone was saying. I just kept nodding and asking Aaron to translate for me every two seconds. By 8:30 p.m., we still hadn't had dinner and Gracie was on hangry tantrum number two. She also would have normally been asleep by then, and starvation mixed with sleep deprivation is a nasty cocktail. By 9:05 p.m. everyone was pretty much drunk and I told Marissa that we would probably need to head home soon because Gracie was so exhausted. She quickly got up and tried to be so accommodating to us and...turned on the oven to PREHEAT IT.

I cried inside. I cried a little out of gratitude for this sweet friend who was trying so hard to make us feel welcome; I cried a little for my headache from trying to understand French; and I cried a little for my tantrum-throwing, delirious child.

After she had cooked all the pizzas, we finally all sat down to eat at 9:45 p.m. Italian pizza is amazing, but to someone starving, it goes to a whole new level. I felt the steam hitting my face as I cut into the pizza, and the smell was enough to intoxicate me. Preparing for my first bite of pizza, I froze when I heard someone yelling.

"*Arrêtez! Arrêtez! Taisez-vous*!!! (Stop! STOP! Be quiet!)." Startled, I looked up at Marissa screaming over everyone to be quiet. "I forgot! Aaron and Alicia pray before they eat. Everyone stop. Aaron—go ahead. Pray." Ummm, awkwardddd. Aaron told her that it was her house and they didn't need to stop for us to pray, but she demanded that he pray. So with everyone watching and waiting for the "show" to begin, Aaron started to pray. No one joined in, but everyone just watched with this dumbstruck smile on their faces like they were watching a circus act they had never seen before. Halfway through Aaron's prayer, a boy asked out loud, "WHAT is he DOING??!"

Aaron stopped momentarily and then hurried to finish the prayer. If we didn't feel like a spectacle before, we sure felt like one then. I heard some snickering, but before Marissa let anyone resume eating, she told Aaron to tell everyone why we pray. I was dying. I just wanted to eat and sleep. At the same time. Is it really so odd to pray before you eat? I've seen it so often elsewhere, but maybe it's unusual here?

Finally, we were allowed to eat. We—the Cardways—inhaled our food while everyone else was still working on their first few bites. Again, we tried to excuse ourselves because it was almost two hours after our kids' bedtimes, but she wouldn't hear of it. She told everyone to hurry up and finish eating so she could get out the dessert for us before we left. At 10:30 p.m. I realized this was a cultural experience, not only for us but for everyone else as well.

We didn't leave until well past 11 p.m. and drove like zombies, with blank stares transfixed on our faces, while our kids whined and cried the whole way home.

THE BISE—PART II

B elgium, October, month six
The *bise* culture is still a really hard one for me to decipher. I'm still trying to figure out the correct usage. I thought my problems were over when I had a rude introduction to it by accidentally kissing the air when going in for a second *bisou*, which is only done in France. Apparently, there is more information to add to the *La Bise 101* pamphlet that has *yet* to be created.

I thought you did the *bisou* whenever you see anyone. Nope. I've been trying so hard to adapt to their culture so they aren't uncomfortable around me, that in the process, I've just made people even more uncomfortable. I have been *bisou*-ing everyone at the school all morning at drop-off, and all afternoon at pick-up. Sometimes even twice at both times. I would see them when we arrived at the school for drop-off or pick-up and *bisou* them. Then I would see them again walking to the car after drop-off or pick-up and *bisou* them. (The muscles around my mouth are in killer shape, by the way). THEN, I see them at soccer, so I kiss hello and again when I say goodbye! I see this particular mom sometimes three to four times a day and the poor woman just thinks I'm a floozy.

Finally, at one soccer practice, I asked all the moms to explain the *bisou* more in depth and what is acceptable. They all laughed like they had been just WAITING for me to ask and explained that it's only when you see them the first time in the day or when you're saying goodbye at a party or someone's house. They explained that I should do it once for the day and then not again at pick-up. We laughed and I thought, *OK, I got this.*

WELL. The next day I was put to the test. I saw a few moms in the morning and *bisou'd* them. Later at pick-up, I saw them all again. *Nope,* I thought to myself, *I've already seen them today, so no* bisou. I looked at all the moms standing. *Oh wait, I haven't seen that one today. Do I kiss only her? I don't really know her though, but I don't want to be rude. Crap. What do I do??* So I walked up and waved "hi" to everyone and looked at the last mom I don't really know and stood there for a second, awkwardly, and then leaned in to *bisou* her. Well, SHE didn't know I had already seen everyone else before and *bisou'd* them that day, so she's feeling extra awkward, as am I, and so I just laughed and had to ask everyone again, "Should I have done that?! I don't know her, but I don't want her to think I'm rude!" However, in my limited French, I asked, "Is it OK? I her don't know, but I don't want that she thinks I'm mean!" The answer is no. NO. I didn't have to kiss her and no she wouldn't have thought I was rude.

Oh my goodness, I can't handle this. I need a notebook to carry with me to keep all these *bisous rules* straight.

My armpits are sweating.

THE FRENCH BLUNDERS
BEGIN—PART I

B *elgium, October, month six*
　　We've been here six months now! All that really means is that there has been plenty of time to embarrass myself. I'm trying so hard to speak more, mostly because everyone here has warmed up to me and wants to make me feel welcome by talking to me. While this is heartwarming, it has provided ample opportunities to look like the village idiot. The other day a mother came up to me and asked—in French—if Will was still playing soccer and if it was still on Tuesdays and Thursdays.

"*Oui, oui, oui,*" I said in my best accent. (I really sold it).

"And is there a match on Saturday?" she said slowly enough for me to understand.

"Oh no, the match is at the butt of practice."

"The butt of practice?"

"Yes, the very butt of practice."

"Oh, that's nice. Mmm-hmmm. OK, see you soon! Have a good day."

I was trying to say the "end of practice," but I mixed up my words and I didn't even realize that until I was falling asleep later that night. It's amazing what moments of clarity one can have in that little space between sleep and awake.

As if I hadn't already publicly branded myself as a simpleton, the next day while waiting for the school bell to ring, I told a mother, in French, that my in-laws came from the States and were *very* tired because it took them fifteen hours to get here from the States by bicycle.

"Bicycle??"

"Yes! By bicycle. Fifteen hours. Soooo long." (Complete with gestures showing my arms stretchingggg as far as they could go and wiping the fake sweat from my forehead followed by a blow of air from my mouth like, 'Whew!'). Insert awkward, silent moment while we are both wishing our children would hurry up and be dismissed from class so we don't have to make small talk anymore. If you have studied French, then you know that the words for "bicycle" and "airplane" don't even sound remotely close, but *you* try remembering all the transportation vocabulary when having a pop-quiz with another parent on the playground.

Finally, the awkward moment won and she turned to me and said, "You are sure? Bicycle?"

"Yes??" I responded hesitantly.

Then she said slowly, "Bicycle? Or is it A-I-R-P-L-A-N-E?"

Dang it.

THE FALL—ROUND II

B *elgium, October, month six*
She fell. AGAIN. I don't know what it is with Ayla and Octobers, but the two just can't seem to get along. Remember when she fell in Turkey? That was also in October.

Ayla was invited by a schoolmate to come and play. I took my other kids to a birthday party and planned on getting Ayla after the party. When picking kids up from a playdate here, it's a whole ordeal. In the States, I wouldn't get out of my car. I'd wait for my child to come out and I'd pull away, waving "thank you" out the window. Here you are always invited in to sit and chat and have a drink. I both love and hate it. The American in me is on a schedule and I don't normally add in an extra twenty minutes for idle chatting. The human in me, however, loves the slower-paced lifestyle and getting to know other people. So I arrived to pick up Ayla and was invited to the back porch to sit and chat while the girls slowly made their way to the house.

This house is an old chateau that sits on at least twenty acres of land. We could see the girls way off in the distance playing under a tree. I chatted with the parents for ten to fifteen minutes and then looked at my watch and started to get up to leave. I could still see the girls way off in the distance, under the tree, and finally yelled out to Ayla to hurry. Her friend started running to the house, but Ayla stayed under the tree. She was so far away, but I could barely see her raise her hand and finally realized she was lying on the ground. I started running out to her. I could hear her friend yelling something in French, but my brain was in emergency mode and not allowing me to understand what she was saying. *My brain must be in emergency mode most of the time.* I ran faster to Ayla and when I got to her, she was letting out the most pathetic, barely audible whimpers. I thought maybe the wind got knocked out of her, but she told me she couldn't move her arm.

I weighed my options in a matter of seconds: If I moved her and her back was broken, it could do further damage, but we were out in the countryside and I couldn't wait an hour for an ambulance. I could take her myself, but I'd have to carry her very carefully to the car so as not to do more damage. I went with my mother's instinct and very carefully picked her up. I swear the adrenaline transformed me into Hulk, because I held her straight as a board with my arms extended and ran back to my van. The parents of Ayla's friend were beside themselves. They were pacing around and panicking. I asked where the nearest hospital was and they stammered out some names, but I hadn't heard of any of those. I knew of the hospital by a military base that was used by English-speaking expats and although it was thirty minutes away, I decided to go there.

Ayla, still whimpering and now lying on the floor of the minivan, was writhing in pain. I'm so grateful for European speed limits. The highways are eighty-five miles per hour in Belgium, and so I didn't really have to worry about the police. I pulled up to the ER parking lot and found the door and elevator down to the right level. Some of my adrenaline had worn off, making Ayla all of a sudden really heavy. I ran into the ER and up to the window and could only get out TWO French words. "*Ma fille! Ma fille!* (My daughter ! My daughter!)." We were immediately rushed back to a room, and Ayla was stripped down and hooked up to IVs and monitors. After x-rays and scans, it was confirmed that she had not only broken her arm, but she had fractured two ribs and punctured her lung. They kept her in the hospital for five days until the little air bubbles in her lungs were gone.

We made it six months in a new country without incident, so this was bound to happen. I feel as if going to a foreign emergency room is a form of expat-hazing that we must all go through—the final stage of being tested to see if we have what it takes to ~~join this fraternity~~ live in this new country.

Hazing complete.

THE HALLOWEEN PARTIES

B *elgium, November, month seven*
Our church in France decided to do a Halloween party, and they were so excited to tell us because everyone over here (in Europe) seems to associate Halloween as being an American holiday. It is not a big thing here yet, but it's starting to be. It was announced several times over the pulpit and people were so excited and gave us the thumbs up from across the chapel, like we personally had something to do with Halloween itself. The church asked us to bring some decorations and to help set up for the party, which we were happy to do. Although we love Halloween, we felt we really needed to go all out because we are the token Americans in the congregation. I brought all my decorations that included everything from scary pumpkins, to witches and skeletons, to spiders. Anything that was decorated with blood or deemed too scary for a church party, I left home. We showed up early to decorate with the family in tow and, of course, in costume. Will had his giant, bloody-mouthed, werewolf mask and costume on. I was wearing an orange shirt with spiders all over it and spider earrings. When we walked in, we noticed it was mostly decorated already...buuuuut with old family pictures everywhere...and everyone from church was in business clothes or Sunday dress. I started to get the nervous giggles and tried to discreetly pull the costume spiders off my shirt. One lady asked if we brought the photos of our ancestors to help decorate. We must have given her blank stares because she said, "Huh? Uh, no? Well, that's OK, you can just put any of your decorations on the table." Looking at the lace tablecloths and crystal punch bowls, my giant scary

spider and spider webs seemed a little out of place among all the nicely framed and mounted pictures of other people's ancestors. After talking with a few people, we figured out they were celebrating All Saints Day/ Dia de los Muertos, but had called it Halloween. The fake candles and family pictures and soft music all of a sudden made a lot of sense. It also explained why we were the only ones ridiculously dressed with spiders and masks.

I literally hate cultural misunderstandings and being uncomfortable. I just giggle like a little girl the whole time as some sort of coping mechanism. Except it's not the cute giggles; it's like a low-throat, deep giggle, much like a thirteen-year-old boy pretending his voice is low. Basically, it's not attractive.

AFTER THE MISUNDERSTANDING at church, we decided to up our game and re-establish why Americans love a spooky Halloween. What better way than to throw a giant Halloween party for twenty-five Belgian kids? If you know us, then you know we are NOT party-throwing people. I literally had to channel my inner Pinterest board and Freddie Kruger. Let's be honest here—we are trying to make friends for our kids. We have no shame. I would pay all of them whatever it takes. We are already associated with Halloween, so why not live up to the stereotype?

I think the kids had a fun time. They all came dressed as demons and zombies, but they also brought birthday presents to all three of our kids, so maybe I wasn't clear in the invitation, but I'd like to think that after the party we reached the "Officially Cool Foreigner" status. Only Monday morning at school will tell.

BELGIUM, MONDAY MORNING

Yep. We're in.

THE FRENCH CLASS

B*elgium, November, month seven*
While most moms at the school are typically polite, but not warm, there is one mom who is SO friendly that I look forward to seeing her any chance I get. It's amazing what a smiling face will do to lift your spirits when you're foreign and living out in the countryside away from anything familiar.

She has also made it her personal mission for me to learn French.

While I AM trying to learn, I still have a mental block. I never realized it would be THIS hard. I had a much easier time with Turkish, and I never even studied or tried. I've since had an *ah-ha* moment and realized it's because I'm a visual learner and Turkish is easier in that sense. You pronounce each letter in a word, the way it is in the alphabet. So once I learned the alphabet, I could pronounce any word. Additionally, there are hardly any exceptions in Turkish. It's almost like math. Just plug in the numbers to the equation and you can figure it out. For me, learning French is like trying to teach a tone-deaf person to harmonize.

In French, it seems there are more exceptions than not, the letters are not pronounced the way they look, and someone kept vowel-vomiting all over the French language and decided to just mash them all together. For example, *queue, feuille, oeil,* and my personal favorites, *jouaient* and *oiseaux*). I mean, seriously, *jouaient*?! I've decided this word must be a product of a sixteenth-century drinking game. Someone was drunk and said, "Let's see if we can fit FIVE vowels between two consonants and make it a word." Needless to say, what I read and what I hear are two completely different languages.

So this sweet mother sent me a flyer advertising a French class for adults located in the neighboring village. It was a free class provided to foreigners living here and while I was willing to go, I desperately wanted to go with someone else. I put it off until she asked, for the fifth time, if I'd been yet.

Finally, on a Monday morning, I decided to just go and get some information so I could tell the mom that I'd been. I had seven things on my To-Do list for Monday while the kids were in school, and this was the first one to check off. I drove to the little village and parked in the church's parking lot, since every typical European town has a church in the center, and I walked around for twenty minutes trying to find the address to this language school.

After a few loops around the town square and saying *bonjour* for the third time to the same old men sitting outside a market, I saw a sign for a school with the same address, except that it was an elementary school. I kept thinking that maybe there was a section for the children and a section for the adults. There was a giant brick wall all around the school with huge barn doors. The white-washed brick wall was at least seven feet tall, but the entrance to the main building with the barn doors was around twelve feet tall. I took a few hesitant steps through the doors and looked around before I backed out. I repeated this action a few more times before finally ventured further into the courtyard looking for an office. After passing the midway point of the sloping courtyard, I was now eye level with the windows and saw all the children in their classes, but no adults. Out of the corner of my eye, a teacher was waving to me through the window. I figured that was the class, but I couldn't find an entrance or an office. A different woman finally entered the courtyard through some hidden door (*why were all the doors hiding?!*) and I asked her where I could find the language school for adults.

"Excuse me, where is it found the school language of adults?" I said in my best French. She shook her head, either implying she didn't know or that she couldn't understand me. *Why not? It was perfectly clearrrr.* She said something indicating that THIS is a CHILDREN'S school (!!!). She was saying this to me as she slowly walked towards me and I was slowly backing out of the courtyard. So I stood outside the barn doors pretending to call someone and googled "How to not feel dumb in foreign situations..." Just kidding! But I did google the address again. I pretended not to notice the woman still walking towards me and I turned my head, pretending to search down the street but really watching her out of the corner of my eye so I could see if she was headed to a hidden front office. She caught me watching her. Obviously my gut reaction was to quickly turn away, which only made me look more suspicious. With my back still turned to her and now "staring" at a very interesting empty sky, I heard the giant barn doors shut (two feet behind me) and a bang of a locking sound. SHE. LOCKED. ME. OUT! I was literally shut out of a school with doors slammed in my face. Seeing the men outside the market watching me, I headed towards my car with tears welled up in my eyes because I absolutely hate being in uncomfortable situations.

I was mumbling to myself, *I don't have time for this. This is not worth it. Who needs French anyway?* When all of a sudden I saw adults! With backpacks! They were walking into another gate along the same brick wall and I practically ran down to catch up. As I walked in and got all of the *bonjours* and *bisous* out of the way, I explained, "I'm just here for information." They spewed rapid French at me, and I'm so proud of myself because I understood 15 percent of what they were saying. Yes, I have an ID; yes, I can fill out a form, etc., etc. After I finished and got ready to leave, assuming they would email or call me when the next session or class starts, she spewed more French at me. While I didn't understand, she motioned for me to follow her and I presumed she was giving me a tour.

From the outside, I hadn't realized what the building was, but now that we started walking the hallways, I realized it was a convent and all the ladies registering me were nuns, in plain clothes. How very modern and new age. We were walking down some long hallways and over some crypts in the floor when she stopped suddenly and opened a large wooden door. The door creaked so loud that the voices I heard on the other side were immediately quiet. Thank you, door, for announcing my entrance. Before I even knew what was happening, she was introducing me to seven other adults sitting there.

"*Bonjour!*" I said.

"*Bonjour et bienvenue,*" they replied in unison.

I started to turn and leave, but I ran straight into the nun. She was not leaving. In fact she turned me around by the shoulders and I felt a little push in my back. She was literally pushing me (kindly) to sit down.

"Oh no, dear. You can sit right there. This is your class," is what I assumed she was saying, although I wasn't sure. *Oh? Oh! We're doing this now! OK, this is happening. It's happening right now.* I could feel the heat rising up my neck, although I am thankful that it never shows or gives me away.

This is the point when I start to become funny. Living overseas is a sure way for self-discovery and I have discovered that I turn into somewhat of a clown when I'm extremely uncomfortable. I make funny jokes in French to divert the tears.

"*Bonjour à tous! Je suis une femme!* (Hello all! I am a woman!)." They laughed and I cried inside. The class continued...excepttttt I realized that everyone in the class speaks French already.

"Um...*c'est la classe pour les débutants?* (Is this the class for beginners?)."

"*Oui! Oui!*"

"Okkkk, *mais tout parler français*? (Okkk, but all to speak French?)." What I was trying to ask was, "Why does everyone already speak French?"

"They are here to learn how to read and write French," the teacher responded, miming the actions for reading and writing. *Was it that obvious I didn't speak French well?*

I've learned that some of them are Belgian and dropped out of school. Some are foreigners that learned French, but never learned how to read and write it. I'm already behind because it started in September AND I am also the only one that barely speaks French. After an hour I'm thinking, *How long IS this class?* Don't worry, I found out. I found out THREE hours later. My brain exercised so hard in those three hours that it lost two pounds.

"See you next week, everyone!" I practically sang when the class was finally over.

"Next week? No, see you Wednnnnnesday. WED-NES-DAY," the teacher slowly enunciated in French while holding up her fingers so I would be sure to know which day she was saying. "Three hours, OK? Have a good day!"

Yep. We're doing this.

THE NERVOUS MOTHER—PART II

Belgium, January, month nine

B The Belgians (and maybe other Europeans as well) treat their children like small adults. Truly. I had heard this, but it wasn't until I got here that I really understood. What most Americans would shield from their children, Belgian children are purposefully exposed to at an early age. This ranges from what their children can watch to how they speak to what they can read—and by that I mean, the books that are literally in the classrooms and school library would no doubt be protested in American schools. Think book-burning level. (When laughing about these differences to a local neighbor she nodded her head stating, "Americans are so prude!")

Our first few months here we visited many book stores in hopes of building a French library to encourage our avid readers to read in French as well. It was only at the second bookstore we visited that we noticed "one of these things is not like the other." (You have to read that while singing it as well.) There was a stack of books—I say stack so one doesn't make the mistake of thinking that maybe it was placed in the children's section by accident—with a price and label indicating the YOUTH section. It was a cartoon book of all the *gros mots,* cuss words, from English and other various languages and their phonetic spellings so children could learn how to say them. I'm still laughing as I write this. It literally listed every word and what they meant and how to use them. I really must be a prude American.

The next aisle over, and in every subsequent bookstore we've been in, there were books on HOW to make babies. Yes. NO. I don't know

144

what to feel. I'm not talking about "Where do babies come from?" I'm talking about literal, anatomically correct cartoons with diagrams and *interactive* pages. I'll let your mind figure out what *interactive* means. Of course I was that crazy woman who whipped out my phone to take pictures of the books just to send home to my siblings and laugh like an immature teenager. Oh how that must have looked to anyone who might have seen me. *Anyway.*

The idea that children are small adults apparently includes the third graders because the big adults at our school decided to send the small adults on a week-long overnight "field trip" to cabins in the woods. While every other parent was thrilled for their little adult-child to have the opportunity, my mind was going to the darkest places and stories of what could happen at overnight camps, especially to my sheltered, non-*gros-mots*-using, unadult-like child.

At the parent informational meeting for the field trip, cell phones were announced as strictly prohibited and we wouldn't be able to speak to them for the entire week. I went back and forth about whether to let Will go. On one hand, he would be able to make more friends and feel like he "fits in" more, but on the other hand, he still doesn't speak the language and could be left out. After hours of contemplating, I (we) decided not to make him stand out any more than he already does and agreed to let him go...on the condition that I speak to the *directrice* of the school first.

I composed a nice little email to her, hit my trusty Google Translate, and copied and pasted (as one does) it into an email. I hit "Send." She responded, and Gmail went ahead and translated it all for me and a meeting was set up. I didn't think this part all the way through. French class teaches you the weather and colors and basic pleasantries, NOT conversations for nervous foreign mothers sitting in a 150-year-old school in the countryside in Belgium trying to explain that her little son was NOT in fact an "adult-child." Lucky for me, this didn't dawn on me until the next day when our meeting actually started.

Imagine the most stereotypical French Parisian woman. The type that prompted the stereotype in the first place. Classy, stone-faced, proper, not a single smile wrinkle...you get the picture. While she had been welcoming and helped us to integrate into the school, she had done it all without displaying a single smile. She was very cordial, but definitely not warm. My default, especially if I'm nervous, is to be overly warm, friendly, and funny, in hopes of hiding my lack of French.

I sat down in her office and when she gestured to go ahead and start, THAT was the point that I realized I hadn't prepared anything and I didn't have Google Translate. Speaking very slowly and translating everything in my head from English to French, word for word, I said, "I'm a nervous mother. This isn't common in the States to send young children on a field trip for a week. He is so young. He is the oldest child in our family, but he is still my baby. Can he take a phone there? He can't speak French yet and no one else there speaks English."

However, using the incorrect words or the wrong accent, what I was in fact saying was:

"I am a mother nervous. It isn't normal in America to send yellow children to a voyage in the fields for a week. He is so yellow. He is the donkey of our family, but he is always my baby. Can he take a phone there? He can't speak French still and anyone there speaks English."

Yeah, go ahead and let that sink in. No wonder I heard crickets. Without taking her eyes off me, she reached behind her and grabbed her phone. *Yes! She understood me!* No, no she didn't. She was calling someone who speaks English. We finished the rest of the conversation on speakerphone with someone who translated for us. I wasn't allowed to send him with a phone and he ended up going and having the time of his life. He felt more a part of the class after that trip and was more comfortable speaking French with the other boys.

However, I'm still a mother nervous.

THE REAL JOB—PART I

Belgium, January, month nine

I got a job! Not an, "Oh bless her American heart—she thinks she's working here" type of job. A real one—albeit extremely part time. I love it. I've taught before, but it's always been with children and adolescents. I was a part-time counselor at a middle school and a case worker at a youth rehabilitation center. When I was in graduate school, I worked at the university's counseling center with college-age students. Well, this week I found myself in a completely different role, sitting at the head of a conference table surrounded by military generals from various European countries to teach Advanced English. First, I'm not an English teacher. There is a big difference between *teaching* a language and *speaking* a language. In the interview, I was upfront and made it very clear that this was the first time I'd be teaching English, but my boss assured me that all the gentlemen already knew English and needed help with advanced English so they could better communicate with other generals and military leaders. Since I had an advanced degree and was comfortable working with members of government and military from my time working on Capitol Hill, she assured me that was all the qualification I needed and gave me an "easy-to-follow" curriculum. Bless her trusting heart.

To say that I was nervous or intimidated is an understatement. The class was to take place at NATO military headquarters and required special access. I parked, walked up, flipped my hair over my shoulder, and waited for my escort like a boss woman. Let's be real, I was literally peeing my pants and my teeth wouldn't stop chattering. An escort was assigned to be with me at all times and signed me in. I put on my best Fake It Till You Make It smile and confidently followed my escort after being scanned for weapons or cell phones. He showed me to the conference room I would be teaching in and left to get the rest of the class members. I set my bag down and tried to decide where to sit. It felt a bit presumptuous to sit at the head of the table, but it was also closest to the whiteboard and I knew I would need it. So I sat down. Then stood up. Then sat down. I couldn't decide what was appropriate. I stood up. One by one these giant men in uniform walked into the room silently and sat down. Seeing that I was the only female, non-military, and shortest-by-a-foot person there, I put on my best teaching face and went for it. I made everyone introduce themselves and realized they are all in Special Ops. That made me pee a little more. I did what I always do when I'm nervous: I started cracking jokes. They were all stone-faced in the beginning, but by the end of the class, we were all laughing so much that someone knocked on the conference room door out of curiosity, just to see what was happening. I had so much fun. I felt like I was in first grade again playing teacher. I wish I could have filmed it just so everyone could have a good laugh, but you'll just have to wait for my stories instead.

THE COMPLIMENT

Belgium, January, month nine

B   I am still taking my French class at the convent and I just learned that the words "*en forme*" mean to be physically in shape. Having been able to consistently work out lately, I have been feeling *en forme*. With this new vocabulary word fresh on my mind, I ran into a mother at the school that I hadn't seen in a while. I asked her how she was doing and she responded with something that included *en forme*. Let me just interject and say that I understand about 40 percent of what's being said to me. I generally deduce the context based on some words I pick out and match them with the person's facial expressions or gestures. So when a sentence isn't long enough for me to pick up on the context, I'm in trouble.

This woman said something short to me, but the only word I really knew was *en forme*. I got a huge smile on my face and looked down at myself and outlined my silhouette with my hands while wiggling my hips and responded in French with, "Is it real? Thank you!" She got a really confused look on her face and I hurried and said goodbye and left. I promptly called Aaron and told him what happened and asked where I went wrong? *Honey, I went wrong when I tried to learn French.* He explained that *en forme* also meant something to the effect of "staying on top of things or going strong." Oh my gosh. So when I asked her how things were going, she had responded by telling me she was staying on top of things while I stupidly responded by giving her a little wiggle. I thought she was telling me I looked "in shape." I am mortified.

Y'all, please be nice to those learning another language.

THE REAL JOB—PART II

B *elgium, February, month ten*
So I'm a couple weeks into my teaching job and although I'm more comfortable, it still makes me laugh. No amount of studying can prepare you for the questions they will ask. Things I never even thought of as a native English speaker. This last week I got a few stumpers. For example, "Can you explain the difference between BUT, NEVERTHELESS, and HOWEVER?" *Ummmm can YOU? Huh? Just pick one and go with it. Whatever rolls off the tongue easier. No? OK.* Curse him for asking that question. At that point I'm cursing the high-security building we are in that doesn't allow computers or phones inside. I'm at a loss when I can't phone a friend or use a lifeline. How did we survive before Google?

Another day I was asked to explain the difference between "despite" and "in spite of." *Just shut up. Stick to the curriculum, dangit.* That was not a part of the lesson. I got flustered and said, "Now you've put me on the spot, which isn't fair because I'm feeling under the weather. The answer is on the tip of my tongue..." which was my great segue into idiomatic expressions and diverting from the original question. Ha! Alicia–1. Class–0. The class should really be titled "Advanced English: Question Deflecting 101."

THE BREATHALYZER

Belgium-French border, March, month eleven

B We've been in Belgium for about seven months now and I've prided myself on knowing enough French to get around, but I'm also in that sweet spot where I can pass off as ignorant if I need to. This is actually a beautiful spot to be in for many reasons. For example, when telemarketers call I just say, "I'm sorry, I only speak English. I have no idea what you're saying," and they usually just hang up. Or when we get randomly stopped at the border because we drive a big enough van to be deemed "suspicious", we just speak English and flash our smiles and yell, "UH-MERICAN" and they get flustered and confused and wave us through. Furthermore, the stereotype of Americans is that we're always smiley and happy and it makes the stereotypical northern European somewhat uncomfortable.

Well, I was on my way home from a church meeting in France and heading back to Belgium when I saw police cars blocking my exit. Apparently this was a day that was publicized in the local news as a "breathalyzer" day, but because I don't read the local news, I was completely unaware. As I was nearing the exit, I saw it blocked by police cars, which caused me to slow down and they motioned for me to pull over. I always speak only English when dealing with police or border control, but these police didn't care one lick about the language barrier.

"I'm sorry, I don't speak French. I don't know what you're saying," I said with my biggest, warmest, friendliest smile and my newfound southern accent.

"It's an inspection for alcohol," he retorted in French. I realized that he knew what I had said in English.

"I'm sorry? I don't speak French?" I said still smiling, but my accent magically disappeared.

After circling and inspecting my van, he walked back up to the window with this little machine unlike anything I'd ever seen before. He said something that I didn't understand and held the machine up. I was starting to piece together what was happening, but I literally had no idea what to do. He motioned for me to blow into the breathalyzer and held it out.

Can I just explain to you how badly I was sweating because I had no idea what to do? Before you laugh and think, "Isn't it self-explanatory?" I'll tell you—NO, it is NOT. Am I supposed to get out of the car? Do I walk the line? Do I take it and blow, or do they hold it? How close am I supposed to get?

I stared at it for a minute thinking, *OK, I can figure this out. Just fake like you know what you're doing.* It had a clear, plastic, circular tube that was about three inches in diameter.

He said something to me again that I didn't understand, so finally I just went for it and opened my mouth as wide as I could to try and get my mouth around the tube while he was still holding it (go ahead and take a minute to visualize this. It was like something that might resemble a teenager's first kiss). He awkwardly stopped me, choking on a stifled laugh, and just told me to blow air at it without even making contact with the tube.

I didn't have to put my entire mouth around it. Gross! What was I thinking?! I was too nervous trying to figure out what he was saying and what I was supposed to do that I didn't take into consideration all the other mouths that could have been on there. I couldn't even look him in the eye while I just blew air at the device and waited for him to allow me through.

I passed, by the way—I'm sure to his surprise after that little *display.*

THE BREAKFAST CLUB

B *elgium, March, month eleven*
Oh man, I've had some doozies this week. I guess I've had it coming and they ALL came this week. Aaron calls my French class "The Breakfast Club." We are like a little family of ten and we get to laughing so hard sometimes. Mostly at me.

In my class there are three Italians, Giorgio and Giuseppina who are in their sixties and seventies and Stephania in her thirties; an older Greek woman, Kalliopi; two Turkish girls, Aysun and Zeynep, in their thirties; and three older Belgians: Jean-Claude, Anna, and Anne-Marie. Giorgio came to work in the mines in the 1970s and speaks French perfectly, but can't read or write it. He is like an Italian version of Santa Claus, except that he is handsy and I find myself wearing big coats every day to add layers so he's just grabbing my coat instead of my waist. Giuseppina is just like an Italian version of Edna on *The Incredibles*. She's no nonsense and has short black hair and glasses. Stephanie is one of my closer friends here. She moved here with her husband and daughter to get away from the mafia, which she says runs everything in the town she's from. She also hinted that it may or may not have been to get away from her in-laws, but it sounds better to say "mafia." She just received her permission to stay in Belgium and she's trying to improve her French.

The two Turkish girls are neighbors and have children that go to the same school as my children. I instantly bonded with them because I speak a little Turkish. Before I learned some French, we only spoke in Turkish. Jean-Claude is one of the Belgians that sits next to me.

He is hilarious and makes the most off-color jokes and comments, but he somehow gets away with it. He smokes an entire pack of cigarettes every morning when we are there. He's really smart, but for some reason asks me the same questions every day and I can't tell if he's joking or if he has some memory loss. Anna is one of the Belgian women there. She weighs all of eighty-five pounds and was in an accident a few years ago that caused memory loss, so she's re-learning to read and write. The final Belgian woman is Anne-Marie, our teacher. She's short and wide with the cutest pixie cut. I've also never seen someone speak so much with their lips and eyebrows. Sometimes I worry that my face is making the same expressions as her and she'll think I'm making fun of her. You know those people, right? The ones whose face is mimicking the speaker when they are listening to an intense story? Yeah, that's me. Anyway, all together we are like a little band of misfits and have formed our own little family.

This week Aysun, one of the Turkish girls, was sitting next to me and asked how much I weigh in front of the whole class. Obviously, given my experiences with the Turks in the past, I didn't think anything of this question and was practically waiting for her to pull out a scale from her bag. So how did I respond? Well, *obviously* I announced my weight to the whole class. (I've come to the point where I believe that if I make it less awkward and just roll with it—rather than give way to my insecurities—then it won't be a big deal.) Except there was silence. They all looked at me and the Turkish girl said, "Um. OK? Cool. But how TALL are you?" She hadn't asked my weight; she had asked how *tall* I was.

Later, during our coffee break, Giorgio came over to me with some pictures. (He doesn't know it, but I've adopted him as my grandpa. Except I might have to wear giant coats for the rest of my life.) He loves to show me pictures of his garden and I try to say what little I know to convey my sincere interest. "Yes. How handsome! Yes. *Magnifique*," or "I love. I love," or "Birds. Mmm. Yes. I love. Garden. Yes. Too cool. I like."

One of the pictures was of his grape vines with gorgeous green and red grapes and I was like, "Oh, you have raisins! You have raisins! I love raisins." But what I had actually said was "Oh, you are right! You are right! I love reason." He just smiled, patted my shoulder, and kissed my forehead. I realized my mistake two days later.

THE REAL JOB—PART III

Belgium, *March, month eleven*
My job teaching Advanced English is going really well. So well, in fact, *they* taught *me* a word today. An English one. I'm not even going to say the word because I don't need to feel even more vacuous, but I have never heard this word in. my. life. We had conversation hour and I would correct certain words or pronunciation while they were speaking. One of them said a word and I said, "You mean this word_____?"

"No," he said, "I mean this word _____."

Then two others said it louder and slower. I said, "Can you spell it for me?" I was about to ask him to use it in a sentence and ask the origin like I've seen kids do in a spelling bee, but decided against it. By now I realized that it was ME because three men were now trying to teach me this English word. He spelled it out on the paper and when I looked at it I had to make a quick decision. Do I bluff and say, "Oh that one!" Or do I humbly and maturely admit my ignorance and hope they don't lose any respect for their "Advanced English" teacher.

Don't even pretend like you don't know what I did.

"Oh, that one!! Yes, of course! I couldn't tell because of your accent. Yes, yes, it's pronounced like this..."

THE FRENCH BLUNDERS—PART II

B*elgium, April, month twelve*

    I thought all my problems would be over when the kids learned French. I thought I wouldn't need to try anymore and they could just translate for me. NO. Now I have a whole new set of problems. The kids will speak in both French and English (in the same sentence) and it can be really confusing, especially because I don't know as much French as they do or because some words sound exactly the same in both languages (remember *faux amis*?).

A few weeks ago, Gracie ended up in the hospital for three days. She had severe dehydration from a virus she caught and as you can imagine it was very traumatizing for her to be x-rayed, get blood drawn, and get IV's put in her. She was a mess. We were supposed to have left for a spring break trip to Portugal, but Aaron took the other two kids and I decided to join them later when they released Gracie...exxxxcept we're in Belgium with socialized medicine and no one is in *any* hurry to let anyone leave the hospital. Where we would have been in and out of the ER in two hours in the States, I was in a room for three days just hanging out in Belgium. I was told she couldn't leave until she had regular bowel movements. The nurses kept giving her this disgusting medicine to loosen her stool because her intestinal lymph nodes were swollen, blocking the intestines, and when they would bring in the medicine she would reject it and scream. One of the times that they brought it in for her to drink, she immediately panicked and started yelling. I calmly explained that we couldn't leave until she drank the medicine and went potty. *Just drink the dang medicine so you can poop and we can go to PORTUGAL.* Apparently, she didn't care for Portugal as much as I did because she started screaming, "I want a pie! I want a pie!"

"OK, baby. Just drink it and I will get you a pie." (Whatever it takes. Don't judge.) She screamed it louder and was visibly shaking. I loudly said that I would get her a pie if she would just drink the medicine! She was full-on hyperventilating for a "pie" and I was then yelling back that I would get her a bloody pie if she would just drink the medicine! Finally, the nurse left and came back with a straw for her. Gracie immediately took the medicine. Um, what just happened. Apparently she had been yelling, "I want a *paille*!!!" which is pronounced the.exact.same.dang.way as "pie" but means "straw." I needed a Xanax after that. And a cigarette. And tequila.

An hour or so later (not enough time for my nerves to have calmed), another nurse came in with more laxatives in a syringe. Obviously it looked like a needle and Gracie had been poked a thousand times so she immediately went ballistic. I was trying to speak to her in French to calm her and also so the nurse would understand and back me up.

I *thought* I was saying, "It won't hurt. No blood, honey. There is no blood. It's just medicine." (Unbeknownst to me I was mispronouncing the word "blood"). The nurse looked at me in this weird and confused way and slowly nodded saying, "Ummm, yeah, there's no 'blood,' honey. No blood. Just medicine," and then looked back at me like, *Is that what I'm supposed to say?* I enthusiastically responded and gave her the thumbs up. Gracie finally trusted us enough to take the medicine from the syringe. The medicine did its job and we were able to leave the hospital a couple days later.

Portugal came and went and weeks passed. One day, Aaron's French tutor was at our house and while I was making dinner, I spilled some spaghetti sauce on me. The tutor asked what it was when he saw my shirt. Thinking I would just joke with him, I dramatically said in

French, "Oh it's just blood...wa ha ha haaa..." in my best French vampire impression, but he just stared blankly at me. Then from across the kitchen Will started laughing and said, "Mooooom you just told him 'Oh it's just a monkey...wa ha ha haaaa.' Hahahahaha!"

I laughed about it and then stopped dead in my tracks and burst out laughing even harder remembering when at the hospital I thought I had told Gracie in French, "There is no blood. No blood." When in fact I was saying, "No monkey, honey. There is no monkey. It's just medicine." And how the nurse looked at me confused and then at Gracie and slowly repeated to Gracie while looking at me out of the corner of her eye, "Ummm, yeah, there's no 'monkey,' honey" and looked back at me like, *Was that right? Is that what I'm supposed to say?*

Silver lining? I bet she'll never forget me.

THE PLAYDATE—PART I

B*elgium, April, month twelve*
My mama heart sang today. As we were leaving the school after pick-up, all these boys were yelling from across the schoolyard to Will, "*Au revoir! A demain*! (Goodbye! See you tomorrow!)." I thought back to Halloween and internally thanked the holiday for existing and improving our social standing here. Then one boy asked if he could come play. And then another. And then another. I've been waiting for this day for eleven months and so I couldn't say no. They were darling and had a great time. They were also a little confused why I was taking so many pictures of them. At one point Will ran into the house to use the bathroom and another boy ran in also and just stood outside the door yelling, "*Tu fais quoi,* Will!? Will!? *Tu fais un peu caca??* Willlllll. *C'est caca,* Will? (What are you going, Will?! Are you going a little poop? Will?? Willllllll. Is it poop, Will?)." Hearing this, I snorted, spraying the drink I was drinking all over the counter and got the giggles. Meanwhile, Will thought it was so weird he just ignored him, which only made the kid ask louder. What in the world? Is this a European thing or is this just specific to this kid? Either way, here's to new friends, new playdates, and new meanings of the word "privacy."

THE FRENCH BLUNDERS—PART III

Belgium, July, month fifteen

B This is the good news with my French: now that I've been here a year, I know enough French to somewhat participate in conversations. The bad news with my French is this: I now know enough French to participate in conversations. Somewhat.

Yesterday we invited a family with four kids from our church over to swim so we could get to know them better. The parents were sitting and chatting by the pool while we watched the kids when somehow our conversation turned to cultural differences between the States and Europe. They were telling us they might move to the States, but they just can't get over how people "hug" there and that it just feels so intimate. We started laughing about the *bisous* and how THAT feels intimate to us. (This whole conversation is in French, by the way.) The wife asked me if I am used to the *bisous* yet and I replied that the *bisous* don't really bother me.

I should have stopped there, but my mistake was continuing to explain why.

I was *trying* to explain how I am a touchy-feely person by nature and I said, "It doesn't really bother me because one of my Love Languages is Touch and so I am touchy with people anyway."

Silence. Followed by a slight "bless-your-heart" nod from the wife and then the biggest, cheesiest, naughtiest smile from the husband.

Apparently the French have *not* read *The Five Love Languages*, because they seemed to completely miss the context. The husband, who can speak English but normally refuses to do so with us, temporarily suppressed his French superiority and explained to me that what I said was, "I'm not bothered because my language of love is touching and so I fondle with others even."

Learn to stop while you're ahead, Alicia.

One step forward, four steps back.

THE FRENCH BLUNDERS—PART IV

B *elgium, September, month seventeen*
I have a new recipe. A recipe for embarrassment, actually. If you ever find yourself immersed in a foreign country or culture, you can totally try this recipe out. It's foolproof. See, my problem is that I don't suppress my humor while trying to learn a new language. In fact, it comes out more. One should just stick to the basics when speaking, and don't try to get fancy and add in humor. I was talking to an older, single man at church and he said something about "Julie." However, my little ears heard *jolie*, which means "pretty" in French. So I said (in French), "No, I'm Alicia, but you can call me 'pretty' if you want!" I winked and pretended to punch him in the shoulder while clicking my tongue.

Then I laughed.

But he didn't.

He just looked down at the shoulder I had just fake punched, trying to figure out what on Earth I was doing. To try and make light of the situation I said, "It's a joke! I'm joking! I'm joking!" But what actually came out in French was, "It's a laugh. I laugh! I laugh!"

Word mix-ups aren't new to anyone learning a new language. I just feel like mine are magnified for some reason. Like the mix-ups purposefully hone in on me to keep me humble. Sometimes I just want to scream, "I am an educated woman and I swear I'm not dumb!" It doesn't matter anyway, because French *hates* me and it would probably come out, "I'm a woman learned and I'm not mute!"

LAST WEEK, I STARTED my French course again after the summer break. I heard that Jean-Claude got a new puppy. After greeting everyone on the first day of class, I turned to Jean-Claude and said, "Jean-Claude! I heard you got a new crapper! Do you have any pictures?!" It took a few minutes (and a few people) to help us figure out that I meant "puppy." *Chiot* = puppy and *chiotte* = slang for toilet, or in other words, "crapper."

Poor Jean-Claude. He's the same person I confused last week. I missed the first few classes of French because I went back to the States for a quick trip. Jean-Claude had messaged me asking me where I was on the first day of class, and I sent him a picture of me with all my siblings explaining that I had gone home for my Dad's sixtieth birthday. He asked if those were my nieces and nephew in the picture with me (I'm the oldest of seven kids) and I responded, in French, "No, I'm the oldest of the family and we are all very spread out." Pay attention, folks, because stupid little accents signs and words that sound similar can change everything. What appeared on Jean-Claude's screen was, "I'm the groin of the family and we are very smeared."

Aîné = oldest child. Aine = groin. Etaler = to spread or smear something.

THE JOKE

F*rance, September, month seventeen*

We flew to southern France for a long weekend to visit Carcassonne. Carcassonne is a famous walled, medieval city that is straight out of a storybook (in fact, they used it as a backdrop for the *Robin Hood Prince of Thieves* movie with Kevin Costner). We take full advantage of long weekends and with twenty-euro flights within Europe, we can afford to pay a little extra for an automatic rental car so I can drive as well. Don't shame me. I'm shaming myself. I beat everyone to it—I DON'T KNOW HOW TO DRIVE A MANUAL. There, I said it. Aaron tried to teach me, but for the sake of our marriage, we don't mention the words "automatic" or "manual" anymore and I just reserve the more expensive automatic cars as rentals. One might ask, "Why doesn't he just drive the whole vacation?" and one would not be wrong in asking that. One would just be smacked for asking that. We tried that. We paid a minimal amount for a manual rental in Ireland and we paid an astronomical amount mentally and emotionally for it. I should write a book called "Tips for a Good Marriage" and it would probably start with something like:

1. Don't try to teach your spouse/partner to drive a manual.

2. Don't mention the words "automatic" or "manual" if you didn't listen to tip #1.

3. Pay the extra amount for a rental car both partners can drive if you want to enjoy your vacation.

In all honesty, this truly has nothing to do with the story, but apparently, I needed to word-vomit and get it all out.

One of the days we were in Carcassonne, we decided to drive up to a beautiful, secluded gorge in the middle of nowhere. The water was absolutely crystal clear and freezing, but our kids swam their little hearts out and by the end of the day, everyone was exhausted and numb. We all zoned out on the way home and there was a moment of quiet that I was relishing while my husband sat in the passenger seat spinning his wedding ring around. You see, while some people have an obsessive habit of playing with a stress ball or picking their nails, Aaron has a habit of always playing with his wedding ring. Constantly. I'm always telling him that he needs to be careful or he might lose it and well, of course, it happened during our rare family moment of Zen. The ring flew through the air pinging various points of the dashboard and finally down a crack in the middle of the seats by the parking brake. Of course I was a bit worried, but it's just a ring, right? He spent the remainder of the drive trying to will his fingers to become child size and seize the ring, but to no avail.

We were returning the car the next morning for an early flight, so it was imperative that we retrieved the ring that night. Furthermore, we were losing daylight fast and knew it would be impossible to find in the dark. The kids were now fighting and whining about how hungry they were. We agreed he would take the kids in and I would go ask the hotel manager if he had some tools since we quickly determined it required taking apart the entire center console.

Putting on my figurative #ForeignWifeBoss pants, I walked into the lobby exasperated and confidently explained in all the French I knew while rolling my eyes, "My husband lost his ring in the car. I'm frustrated. Do you have any tools I could borrow?"

However, what actually came out of my mouth was, "My husband lost his wand in the car. I frustrated. Do you have tools I could borrow?"

He looked at me while clearly trying to maintain a straight face and said, "Wand, ma'am?" It still didn't dawn on me that I had mixed up the words so I thought he was saying, "Ring, ma'am?"

I answered, "Yes! His wedding ring! (Yes! His marriage wand!)." I was already flustered, sweating, and kind of laugh-growling. I have no doubt that he thought I was under the influence of something. Finally, he politely told me to hold on and he went to get his maintenance guy, who was standing just outside. I stood there watching them through the window and saw them talking and looking in my direction with their very pronounced French facial expressions. (Have I already explained the French facial expressions? The French talk with their face. They cannot have a conversation without using their eyebrows, tilting their head to the side, and raising their shoulders. What often accompanies these gestures is a downward turn of the mouth and the release of some air through the tight lips, almost like blowing a raspberry in the air. Go ahead and YouTube it now that you've tried it while reading this. I know you did.)

I can only imagine what the manager was saying to the maintenance guy. *So we have this foreign lady staying here who has clearly been drinking too much and she's going on about some unseen husband and his "wand." We need good reviews, so can you just go and pretend to help her?*

After their "gestured" conversation, the maintenance guy came over and said something I didn't understand, and I motioned for him to follow me. He really thought I was crazy now. We walked silently across the endless parking lot and finally got to the car. I opened the car and pointed to the parking brake and slowly enunciated in French, "The wedding ring! There! (The marriage wand! There!)." His 6'4" plus frame (I know this because he was definitely taller than my husband's height) crouched down to the crawl into the tiny rental car. He (feigned to) look around and told me he couldn't see anything (probably because he was looking for a wand) and I agreed, saying,

"Yes, I know because it's so small!" making the gesture with my own fingers for "small."

He finally backed out of the car and looked at me kindly—or sympathetically—and asked, "Ma'am, where *is* your husband?" I crossed my arms, snorted, and pretended to be a stereotypical angry wife saying that he was in "big" trouble. but I didn't know the word for trouble so I dramatically announced, "Oh hohhh—He is BIG punished. Very bad," with an eyebrow raised, winking, and nodding my head like, *You get it, huh? Your wife would be mad if you lost your wedding ring also!*

His uncomfortable laugh didn't indicate to me one way or another if he was on the same page, so I asked if I could borrow his tools. Being the justifiably skeptical man he appeared to now be, he told me that he would just take it all apart himself. *I will NOT give the crazy foreign lady a weapon when she's admitted she's 'BIG' punished her invisible husband.*

While I was breathing over his shoulder because I was NOT about to pay for any damages to the rental car—it hit me. I'd been saying "wand" and not "ring"!! I started laughing out loud and said, "Excuse me, sir, I'm so embarrassed! My husband didn't lose his wand! He lost his JOKE."

"His joke?"

"Yes! His joke. You see, I'm learning French. I thought the word was 'wand.' No, no he lost his joke."

I went from confusing the word "wand" for "ring" to confusing the word "joke" for "ring." Can we just take a moment of silence for this poor guy? The poor guy. Poor, poor guy. I'm not crazy, you're crazy.

He took apart the entire console of a rental car for a crazy lady with a missing, punished husband and his lost joke/wand. He looked at me like, *Please. Please get the help you need,* but what he said was, "I don't see anything, ma'am. I'm sorry."

I asked if I could look and I got in there and felt down in the crevices of the exposed console area, really digging deep, and I

FOUND it! I pulled it out triumphantly and he just stared for a minute before he started laughing, shaking his head, and waving his arms in a crossing motion.

"Your husband's RING!!! He lost his RING. Not his JOKE. Not his WAND! His ringggg."

Ring = bague.

Wand = baguette.

Joke = blague.

Hopeless = Alicia.

THE UNDERWEAR

B *elgium, November, month nineteen*
　　Apparently, word mix-ups run in the family and don't just happen to me. I apologize in advance to my children and future posterity. You got it from me, not Aaron's side.

Will told me this morning that he was called out for using the wrong word. I won't lie when I say I felt a little proud, a little sad I missed it, and so sorry he has the gene. As part of P.E. in Belgium, students are sent by bus to a pool for swim lessons starting at age three. It's part of the curriculum and imperative for children to learn how to swim from a young age. Awesome, right? We are in Europe and we already know how they feel about communal toilets, so obviously there are communal changing rooms (genders are separated after preschool). Using the toilets with everyone was very easy for my kids to get used to, but not the changing rooms. It was definitely easy to pinpoint the Americans since my kids practically pulled a muscle trying to change without allowing an inch of skin to show.

We've been here over a year and they're all finally used to it. Will happened to have swim class yesterday and came home telling me that he's never been so embarrassed in his life and it's obviously all my fault. Already feeling really defensive, I asked him to tell me what happened. Will was in the locker room changing and talking with the other boys and noticed he couldn't find his underwear. He said, out loud, "Dang. I've lost my *culottes* and can't find them." Laughter immediately erupted and Will, ever confused, pretended to laugh right along. The boys didn't stop laughing. Finally, someone explained that

171

Will had used the words for "panties" instead of "underwear." The. Poor. Kid. It doesn't help to already be the foreign kid, but then to make a mistake like that in the LOCKER ROOM of all places??!

He was right, it was my fault. I've only ever used the word *culottes* for "underwear" because that's what my girls taught me (and they learned it from the other kids at the pool). So I will say things like, "'Today is swimming, don't forget your extra pair of *culottes*" and *wa-la*, a French blunder is born and passed on to Will.

You're welcome, son. Embrace it.

THE SMELL

B elgium, March, month twenty-three
The French universe still hates me and is determined to squash me. I see this pregnant woman every day at school pick-up and we usually just say our *bonjours* and do our *bisous* and go on our way. Lately, it's quite evident by her waddle that she is at the last stages of her pregnancy. The other day after we said *bonjour* and I gave her a *bisou*, I stopped her and asked her how she was feeling. In return, I got a horrid look. Assuming she was showing me how she felt with her face, I mimicked her look to show my empathy and compassion. She never answered me, so I just asked again and this time I slowed it down. "How. Are. You. FEELing?"

She still didn't respond, and I started to get nervous. Moments of awkward silence passed and then a light went off in her head and she smiled and told me she was tired, but that the baby was almost here.

When I got in the car with my kids, I asked them to confirm how you say, "How are you feeling?" WRONG. I had directly translated English into French when they don't use the same expression we do to ask that question. So after we had said "hello" and kissed on the cheek, I immediately stopped her and said, "How you smell!" Then when I slowed it down it was really, "How. You. SMELLLLLL."

Why, French? Why do you hate me so?

I drove home embarrassed and deflated. On my drive-of-shame, passing all the usual cows in the beautiful countryside, I noticed an abnormally large cow out in the field sitting on its haunches just as a dog would sit. I laughed out loud and thought, *I feel you cow, I feel you.* You see, like the cow trying to pose as something it's not, I'm desperately trying to belong in this beautiful country and speak a language that my brain and tongue are just not meant to speak.

I am the cow, sitting awkwardly, so out of place, in the beautiful countryside.

THE LUXEMBOURG
CEMETERY—PART II

B *elgium, Memorial Day, May, month twenty-five*
In honor of Memorial Day, today seems like the perfect day to tell this story. It's a long one, but it's so beautiful. I haven't shared it until now because I couldn't properly express the impact it made on me. I still can't, but I'll share it anyway.

I love genealogy. No really, like, I *love* it. Not only do I love doing it for my family, but I love doing it for others as well. It's like a puzzle and I get to go on a treasure hunt and put in some missing pieces and connect them together. Like detective work. Basically, my hobby is to be a detective. Because I love genealogy, I also love going to cemeteries. I love trying to picture each person and what their personality could have been like. So pair my love of genealogy with my obsession of all things World War II, and you can pretty much guess my European bucket-list items.

Last summer we stopped in Luxembourg on one of our trips. We visited the World War II American Cemetery and it was such a beautiful and spiritual experience. I cried when thinking of all these young boys who died and never made it home to their families and of all the mothers who never got to see their babies again. That kind of hurt never leaves a mother's heart. I kept imagining my own son, who was living and breathing and walking through the rows and rows of headstones, leaving and never getting to see him again. So basically I was just a sobbing, snotty mess. Feeling helpless, I wondered how I could use my detective skills to honor them and somehow link them back with their families—maybe just add them in their family tree on Ancestry.com or FamilySearch.org. I couldn't bring them back to be buried with or near their families, but I could digitally link them together. My small token from one mother to another.

Well, there were 5,000 graves and obviously I couldn't get all their information, so I stopped amongst the headstones and had a quick prayer. I prayed to know who was ready and wanting to be found and linked to their family tree. I started walking and stopped at two separate headstones, took pictures, and we left. A month or two later I finally looked at our trip pictures, saw the two headstones from the cemetery, and remembered what I committed to do.

In order to add these names, I needed to find their family tree. In order to find their family tree, I had to go through public records and find family members that might already be in a family tree. It's not necessarily a quick task and I didn't have a lot of time, so I prayed in my heart about which of the two I should start trying to find. I was drawn to one of the two—his name was Leroy. I started to look him up and found his draft card, which led me to his birth certificate which showed his parents' names. I looked up his parents to see if they were already in Ancestry and they weren't. I had to do more digging through online records and find his grandparents' names. The first two grandparents were not already in Ancestry, but BINGO, the third one I searched for was already there. From that grandmother, I was able to put in Leroy's parents and then add Leroy as their child. I saw in one census record that Leroy had two brothers, one of which I discovered had fought with Leroy, only his brother came home after the war and Leroy didn't. Leroy died at just nineteen years old fighting in the Battle of the Bulge.

I noticed that Leroy had another brother who was listed on earlier censuses, but missing on later censuses. At this point I was completely committed to Leroy and his family. It was late and Aaron kept telling me to come to bed, but soon Aaron was snoring and I was still sitting at my computer, unable to stop until I found Leroy's little brother. After an hour of digging I found him. He had died in a different state at a hospital at a very young age. I added the brother to the family tree and finally sat back to look at Leroy's tree. I felt at peace and "released" from the task I set out to complete. I mentally said goodbye to Leroy and his profile picture that I had uploaded from his draft card.

Months went by and one night I was up at two in the morning with Gracie as usual. (She is up several times a week with growing pains, but that is a story and diagnosis for another day.) In order to stay awake while rubbing her knees or shins, I usually read the news and check my email until she falls asleep and I can go back to bed. That night I hopped on the FamilySearch app to play around. The app has interactive features I was playing with when I saw a new one that said: "Map My Ancestors." I clicked on it and a world map popped up with little dots of pictures of all my ancestors that were near me. I could see ancestors in England and Ireland (it showed the closest ones to me since we are in Belgium) and when I zoomed out to see more, I got really confused. I thought I clicked something wrong, because there was a little face there on the map that I HAD JUST PUT IN two months ago. The face on the map was Leroy in the Luxembourg American Cemetery.

You can imagine my complete bafflement when I saw "Map My Ancestors" and his picture popped up. I thought I had made a mistake or that it only popped up because I had been the one to put him in and maybe that accidentally showed up on my map. It hadn't done that for all the other non-related persons I've added to FamilySearch, so this one confused me. After staring at it for a minute, I clicked the name of Leroy and selected the option to see how we are related. Sure enough cross my heart and hope to die – I kid you not...we are distant cousins. I was literally jaw-dropped and dumbfounded. I signed out. I signed back in. I checked it again. Twice. WE ARE RELATED.

Slowly, doubt set in and I thought, *Well if you go back far enough, we're all probably related, right?* I checked three other random names of men buried in the same cemetery and found no distant relationship whatsoever. I sat there tearing up, unable to fully comprehend or grasp how this was all beautifully orchestrated, but I also felt an overwhelming sense of gratitude that it had happened. The other side is so much closer than we realize.

Happy Memorial Day and thank you to all those who have served our country and especially to Leroy.

THE PLAYDATE—PART II

B *elgium, June, month twenty-six*
It's 9 a.m. and I'm already 0 for 2 today. I thought that after two years I was in the clear with embarrassing foreign experiences, but apparently I was wrong. Let me just say that living in a foreign country is great and all, but it comes with a price. There are different levels of being an expat and your experiences vary greatly depending on which level of expat you are. Some expats only live around other expats and never integrate into the community or learn the language. Other expats integrate so much that you never would guess they're originally from another country. I'd say we are somewhere halfway to "full-blown expat." We know other expats and can get some American items at a nearby commissary (i.e peanut butter and brown sugar), but we live nowhere near any other expat or English-speaking person for that matter. In this lay the challenge.

After a break, the schools slowly started opening up in phases. According to the school website, Ayla's grade started school again today. It was like pulling teeth to get her to go again because it's her brother's birthday and she desperately didn't want to miss any of the festivities. There were a lot of tears and stress all the way to school, but I gave her my ten-minute-long pep-talk and "we won't do anything without you" speech.

It was beautiful and warm enough to be outside, which made it even harder for her to go back to school. I parked the car and started to walk her to her class. Feeling more chipper, she skipped up to the school so excited to see her other friends in the courtyard. We walked up to the gate and the never-smiling principal demanded in a monotone voice, "What are you doing here?"

"Ummm, I bring Ayla to school?"

"No. Ayla's grade starts Thursday. Today the preschoolers start. I know it was probably hard for *you* to understand, but we posted it on the website."

"Um, OK. OK! No problem!" I practically sang to her, trying to hide my embarrassment and never wanting to give others the satisfaction of seeing my pride sliiiip away. Ayla, normally the most confident child ever, was equally embarrassed and practically ran back to the car. So much for vowing to never embarrass my kids.

Don't worry, it gets better. Or worse. Depends on who you are. So we were in the car on our way home and I got a call from a number I didn't know. Normally I don't answer because if my French is rough in person, you can imagine it's even worse on the phone. I rely so much on my charades to get me through a conversation and obviously a phone call doesn't permit that luxury. In the future someone should create that option—like closed-caption with description. *Caller is flailing her arms like a bird. Caller is pretending to read a book. Caller is doing the charades for waking up in the morning.* I think it's genius, and you heard it here first.

Anyway, I decided to answer the phone and heard, "Hi! _____ the *mamie* (grandma) of Camille. _____ mom ____ work today and I'm here all day____and so we _____ if Ayla ____ come and play." Every conversation on the phone is like this for me. I understand half of the words and fill in the blanks for the rest and based on what I've strung together, I formulate a response.

Now let me back up a little and give some context to this situation. This invitation was so unexpected but so welcome given the fact that I've had some uncomfortable situations with the mother of the girl. She is not the warmest person and more of a passive-aggressive person by nature (she must be related to the principal). Her daughter is in Ayla's class and they get along so well, but I've heard the mother chastise her daughter for not getting the grades that Ayla does and "French is not even her first language!" I've invited her daughter over several times and her mom always comes up with an excuse, but I see her daughter going on other playdates. The mother is cordial, but cold with me and it's very clear she is not in favor of our daughters playing. Her daughter has asked me if Ayla could come over a few times while we were all standing outside of the school and her mother quickly grabbed her and spoke in such rapid whispering French that I couldn't understand, but Camille just looked down at her feet. One time, the mother did allow Camille to come over for Ayla's *anniversaire* with the rest of Ayla's classmates. It probably didn't help the fact that our company-rented house happened to be very nice and her assumption that all Americans are wealthy may have added to the lack of things we have in common.

Anyway, the girls love each other, so I was elated that Ayla was actually invited over to Camille's house even if it was just by the *mamie*. Progress!! I made a U-turn and drove straight to Camille's house. The *mamie* had said that it didn't matter when Ayla came over and if we were in the car already, she could come right then, even though it was 8:30 a.m. As we pulled up, the van crunched on the rocks lining the driveway and I saw Camille slowly come to the window after hearing our car. She saw Ayla and with an excited look on her face, she disappeared and two seconds later the front door opened. Ayla couldn't open the van door fast enough and she leaped out of the car like a gazelle. The two girls greeted each other in typical seven-year-old fashion, with squeals, hugs, and jumps.

Ayla exclaimed, "I'm so excited to play today!"

"This is so nice of you to invite her over, Camille," I said once the squeals subsided. Camille got a confused look on her face and while scrunching her nose, she said, "What??" I cursed myself for ruining what I thought must be a surprise. It could have been that she had just woken up, since she was standing in her pajamas, and had yet to learn from her *mamie* that Ayla was coming. I relayed to her what her *mamie* said, embarrassed to have ruined the surprise. Camille just stared at me and scrunched her nose even more (that nose can scrunch!) and told me her *mamie* wasn't even there, but her mom was. Next thing I knew, she disappeared and ran to get her mom. Everything happened in slow motion then.

Realizing I must have made a mistake and before I could make a run for it, the mom (*awkwarddddd*) came to the door in her pajamas, coffee in her hand, and appeared so perplexed. So I reluctantly said again (which ended up turning into a question), "Thank you so much for inviting Ayla over? She's so happy to see Camille?"

"I have no idea what you're talking about," she bluntly whispered with quarter-size eyes while ever so slightly shaking her head. All I heard was, "Bless your ever-loving crazy, foreign, heart." My mind was racing so fast that I forgot Ayla was even there until I felt her pinned to my back, hiding. At this point, I would have given my left arm to just disappear. I stumbled all over my words in French and practically backed away to the car all while pretending to be cool and blowing kisses with an air of, "My mistake! No problem! Doesn't bother me, nope! I'm cool! Ain't no thing!" But really, I was DYING—because I just mistakenly showed up at this particular woman's house at 8:30 a.m. and thanked her for inviting us over. Of ALL the women it could have been.

As I practically peeled out of the gravel driveway, still waving and with an overly exaggerated smile on my face, Ayla confessed, "Mom, I've never been so embarrassed in. my. life," and I know I've ruined her childhood now.

So who had called me? I clearly am not the one who should be coordinating things on the phone, so because Ayla speaks French better than I do, I made HER call the number back.

It turns out that it was the NANNY of Louis and his little brother. The NANNY's name was Camille. It was not the MAMIE of

CAMILLE. Have I told you that French hates me? I laugh-cried all the way to Louis's house and Ayla would NOT get out of the car. When I finally convinced her that we weren't wrong this time, she slid out of the car like a jellyfish (the gazelle died back at Camille's house) and hid behind the bush until I confirmed that we were at the right house.

One year left.

THE FRENCH BLUNDERS—PART V

B*elgium, July, month twenty-seven*
    Sometimes I don't even know why I try anymore. It's been two years, and I *really* need to learn to "verify" before using words I hear in French. I hear *coucou* used all the time at the school between the kids and some of the moms. Some moms have even said *coucou* to me. It's such a fun word to say and rolls right off the tongue. Go ahead and try it. It has, in fact, become one of my favorite words to use since learning French. I had always assumed it was like "Heyyyy!" Or "Hey you!" So I used it. A lot. For almost two years now. I've used it with my boss, my landlord, our church's bishop, the cashier at the grocery store, and even when meeting people for the first time. The other day I was emailing someone for Aaron while he was driving and read the composed email back to him. I had used *coucou* to start a friendly email and Aaron immediately stopped me and kind of laughed and said, "Oh, don't use that. That's only used between kids or friends who are being playful. It's the equivalent of 'peek-a-boo.'" Ummm What. The. Heck. Whyyyy? My poor landlord who opens every text and email from me that starts with "peek-a-boo!"

Why stop there? I've got many more where that came from. When I picked up my kids from school yesterday I saw a woman with a new haircut, including new bangs. Obbbbviously I started my sentence with *coucou* and said, "*Coucou*! I love your bangs! They make you look so young and change your look!"

She acted like I didn't even compliment her. Rude. She just paused and looked at me and then we talked about something else. Feeling like something was a little off, I asked my kids in the car how you say, "Hey! I love your bangs! They make you look so young and change your look!" Turns out I did NOT say the correct thing. "Bangs" in French is *une fringe*, and I had used the word *singes*, which happens to be "monkeys." (The French word for "monkeys" is literally going to be the death of me here.) According to my children, what I had in fact said to her was, "Peek-a-boo! I love your monkeys! They make you young and change your face!" Bless her for just trying to go on with the conversation and not make me feel dumb.

The worst part is that I can't stop her the next time I see her and explain that I made a mistake. If I can't even tell her I like her new bangs, how can I *explain* to her I had a "word mix-up"?

THE FRENGLISH

B *elgium, August, month twenty-eight*
    Frenglish is in full swing at our house! This is not something we prepared for or thought of when our kids first started speaking French. They will be speaking in one language and mid-sentence switch to the other language. The little neurons in my brain can't fire fast enough to make that switch with them. Gracie, the youngest, does it the most. She will say things like, "Don't you dare *jeter dans la poubelle* (throw it in the trash)." Or "*Je sais que* you're right there, Will! *Ne me fais pas* scared! (I know that you're right there Will! Don't scare me!)." Some of the ones I've heard and written down in the past week are:

"Mom! I'm *presque* finished!" (*Presque* = almost)

"Can we go to the *magasin* for to buy *pain au chocolat* ?" (Can we go to the store to buy chocolate bread?)

We've noticed that they also form English sentences like they're constructed in French. For example, if a French speaker wants to emphasize their opinion on a subject, they would say, "*Moi, je pense...*" which literally translates to "ME, I think..." while in English we would just emphasize the "I" and say, "*I* think..."

Our kids construct English sentences like French sentences. Another example we hear all the time is, "Are we going to soon eat?" Normally a native English speaker would just say, "Are we going to eat soon?" but now that they're learning French, their sentence structure has changed in English. A while ago I asked what score Will and Ayla got on a quiz and they responded with "A 10 on 10!" (In French it's 10 *sur* 10). While in English we would say, "10 out of 10." It's really quite fascinating to me how the brain works. I wonder if they would have done that had they grown up bilingual with two parents speaking different languages.

Remember how I said that my brain can't make that switch fast enough sometimes? It definitely provides for some hilarious miscommunication. The other day Will was talking to me while I was making lunch. He was going on about something and I was only halfway listening. My ears perked up when he said, "Mom. This morning I saw a pube on the TV and..." He stopped short when he saw the disgusted look on my face. "Mom? Do you know what a pube is?"

"Ummmmm yes, I do. Do YOU know what a pube is?"

"Yeah, of course, but why are you looking at me like that?"

"Because that's GROSS, Will! Why was it on the TV?"

"Mom. Pube? Like *publicite?* Do YOU know what that is? It's like, uh...(searching for the English word)...a commercial!"

The entire time I had heard "pube" when in fact he was saying *pub* in a French accent that sure sounds a whole lot like "pube" to my little English ears.

"Oh yep. Uh-huh. Yep, that's exactly what it is. Mmm-hmmm."

I'm still laughing.

THE MOM FAIL

Belgium, September, month twenty-nine

B A few weeks ago I heard a new song called "*Parlez-vous Français*" and was totally digging it. I've been jamming out to it at home and when I picked the kids up from school I played it for them. They got embarrassed looks on their faces and laughed nervously. Assuming that they were going through what every child does when they see their parents sing and dance, I teasingly said, "What?! I love it! It's good! This song isn't cool enough for you because it says, 'Do you speak French?' Come on, it's cool!" They all looked at each other laughing, rolled their eyes, and said, "Just please don't play this in front of our friends!" Obviously, this was a perfect opportunity to embarrass my kids, so of course I did at the soonest opportunity.

The kids at school know that they can ask to come for a playdate and I will always let them, so it wasn't long before I had a car full of kids coming over after school. I turned on "Parlez-vous Français" and blasted it in the car. I received a plethora of head shakes and red faces. Then I did it again a few days later with a new group of friends and received the same forehead slapping reaction. I was thoroughly enjoying my parental right to embarrass my kids.

I hit repeat and kept it going. Finally from the rearview mirror I asked my kids in front of their friends, in English, "What?? I don't get it! It's not *that* bad. Why are you literally angry with me??"

"Mom. Stop. It's embarrassing! The singer keeps saying to 'take off all your clothes'!"

I whipped my head around and yelled, "What?!?! I've been playing that song for weeks! [*Gasp*] AND around all your friends!"

"I knowwww. We TOLD you it was embarrassing and not to play it in front of our friends!!"

The chorus of the song had been too fast for me to understand and I completely missed it. Such a mom fail, and now I'm the dirty American mom.

THE FRENCH BLUNDERS—PART VI

B *elgium, October, month thirty*
We've been here over two years and Gracie still has a hard time going to school sometimes. When I walk the kids to class each morning, I can hear Gracie (now five years old) talking to herself under her breath saying, "I can do this. I can do this. We do hard things. I can do this." It breaks my heart. I've asked her several times why she has a hard time and although her explanations change, currently it's because it's "too loud" in the classroom and cafeteria—which I can attest to. I don't know if it's the small school rooms or the old building and not a lot of insulation or carpet to absorb the sound, but it IS so loud.

Gracie hates loud noises, and school is no exception. Finally, after enough complaints and begging to be able to wear the "earmuffs" to school, I relented and gave in. She literally went to school with neon-green, industrial safety earmuffs that I wear when mowing the lawn. So when I dropped her off at school, I tried to explain to her teacher why my five-year-old was wearing neon-green earmuffs that covered the entire side of her face. I explained that she is sensitive to the noise. I said (in French), "Is it OK if she wears these today? There is too much noise and her ears hurt." The teacher looked outside, across the front lawn and naturally, I looked to see what she was looking at. Why was she looking outside? Looking back at me, the teacher finally smiled and said, "*Bien sur*," of course, but her eyes were saying something else I couldn't grasp.

Gracie wore them for the next couple of days and a few parents made funny comments and I would explain that she's really sensitive to the "noise" and they all did the same thing the teacher did—they looked around outside. *Whatever. Maybe it's cultural.* (No, Alicia, it's never cultural. It's just YOU).

A couple of weeks have gone by and yesterday we went on an early morning walk in the woods. It's fall and the air is so crisp and quiet. Yesterday was particularly foggy and you couldn't see more than twenty feet ahead of you—which makes for the perfect setting just before Halloween. We were practicing French as a family and I asked my family how to say "fog" in French. They responded with *brouillard* (pronounced bree-yar). I said, "No, that's the word for 'noise'. What's the word for 'fog'?"

"That IS the word for 'fog,' Mom. *Bruit* (pronounced bree-y) is the word for 'noise.'"

I just stood there and started laughing. It dawned on me that I had told all those people that my daughter was wearing safety earmuffs because of all the "fog" around. No wonder everyone was looking around. #blessmyheart #itsbeentwoyears #whycantigetthis

THE VIOLENT AMERICANS

B *elgium, March, month thirty-five*
One of the questions we have been asked the most while living here is: What is different between America and Belgium? Oh, the list could go on and on, but inevitably, and embarrassingly, violence and school shootings are always brought up in the conversation. Everyone has their own theory about why there are so many school shootings in the States, ranging from legal gun possession to violence in the media (i.e. video games, TV, movies, etc.). Someone once mimicked Americans at a group dinner we were attending and said, "Oh sure, you're all upset if there's a little nudity, but no one bats an eye at torture and abuse in movies." I have to say he had a point. I remember when the movie *Titanic* came out and there was some fuss about bare breasts being shown and it was only rated PG-13. Years later when I was working as a junior high school counselor, the principal asked me to talk to a group of kids who were openly making lists to enter into a contest of various ways to torture people for the next *Saw* movie. Like I said, he had a point.

Recently we had Futsy over for lunch after church. Futsy is our adopted family member here. She's a refugee in France from Eritrea and when we met her at church, we instantly fell in love. She's a sixty-year-old woman who has more love to give than a cuddly kitten and we love her so much. Sometimes after church we bring her back to Belgium to spend the day with us before taking her back to her apartment in France. Since Eritrea was colonized by Italy, she cooks a mixture of Eritrean and Italian food, and it's to die for. As we were sitting for lunch, we started talking about America and, of course, violence came up. Aaron and I *tsked* about how horrible the violence is and our ideas of how to prevent it and what causes it. I went on and on about worrying about school shootings and the safety of our kids. I may have mentioned how parents need to be more involved and be better examples. We can be pretty open with Futsy because our two cultures are completely different and it's not political between us at all.

After lunch, we all sat down to watch some family home movies, which is what we usually do on Sundays. Our kids chose a random year (they're all categorized by year) and I hit play. THE FIRST VIDEO to come up showed me with a gun in my hand, at a shooting range, shooting at a PICTURE OF SOMEONE. I took a shot and turned toward the camera and said, "Look, babe, I got him in the neck!" *Someone put me out of my misery right now. I am* dying. Aaron and I immediately squeezed each other's hands so hard and had the same immediate idea to create a diversion. We both started yelling and talking nonsense and creating such a commotion that everyone turned toward us and we directed their attention out the window long enough for me to hit every button on the remote to just turn the IMAGE OFF. The image of me with a gun in my hand shooting at a paper target with a photo of a person on it. Yeah, I just ate all my words about violence and parents' responsibilities and *blah blah blah*. I ate them and vomited them and ate them again.

I then tried to backtrack, tripping all over my words, and explain that shooting ranges are a sort of entertainment or sporting activity. I was digging the hole even deeper. I explained that for Aaron's birthday one year, I surprised him by taking him to a shooting range. I might as well have said in my most innocent and flightiest voice, "That's what we do as Americans! We shoot at targets for fun and take our kids there and I have NO idea why gun violence is even an issue!" (Did you just read that with a voice two octaves higher? Because every time I read this, the little voice inside my head slides up the octave scale. I'm practically squeaking.) Meanwhile, there have been wars in Eritrea and Ethiopia for years and gun violence is no "Saturday afternoon family fun."

I literally have never been so embarrassed. Yes, we do love hitting targets and going to shooting ranges. No, I don't let my kids play any video games that shoot anything. Yes, we have a BB gun. No, we don't have a real one. I feel like we *royally* confused her and I'm hoping that since English is her fourth language, she will just assume something was lost in translation. Fingers crossed.

THE OLD MEN

Belgium, April, month thirty-six

Often I go walking with Stephanie and Aysun after we drop the kids off at school. We take different routes through the villages and pastures and along the canal. We walk a few miles talking and laughing in our broken French since it's our common language. It's amazing how much we can talk about when we only have an intermediate level of French. We laugh, we cry, and we support each other. Sometimes I'm not sure what we're crying about, but they cry, so naturally, I cry.

Today we took a new route and I was having a *moment*. I got caught up in the vast open skies and the cows mooing in the pastures and the crooked steeple from a 600-year-old church in the distance. I kept gasping and trying to explain how much I loved the history and antiquity. Soon we were passing a *really* old stone house with the number 1862 formed by colored rocks cemented into the side of the house. I stopped, slapped my legs, and proclaimed to my friends, "I just LOVE really old homes." Knowing that they grew up in Turkey and Italy, where old homes are just a part of the landscape and nothing out of the ordinary, I continued to elaborate.

"You see, old homes are *rare* in the States. There are a few, but not many. Old homes have so much character! People just want new homes and so they destroy old ones. It's really sad."

It was silent as we all kept walking and I finally turned to them and said, "Old homes? You don't like?" Stephanie looked at me and said, "*Hommes?*"

"Yes! You don't like?..." And then it hit me. I had said the English word *home* (instead of *maison*) with a French accent, which made it sound like *homme*, which is their word for *man*. I literally had said, "I just LOVE really old men. Old men are so rare in the States! There are a few, but not many. Old men just have so much character! People just want new men so they destroy the old ones. It's really sad."

We all just burst out laughing. I explained the word mix-up and they understood—having been in similar situations while trying to learn French. Finally, I had someone to laugh with and share my blunders with! But noooo, I couldn't just stop there—I had to keep going. I was sweating from laughing so hard and said, "I have luck that I put _____ because I am vacuuming!" I didn't know the word for deodorant, so I just acted out myself putting on invisible deodorant but looked like a gorilla scratching his pits. Apparently, I didn't know the word for "sweating" either because I mixed it up with "vacuuming."

I will not miss these blunders, but oh man does my heart hurt when I think about leaving these girls...and these old men and vacuuming gorillas.

How have I survived this long with my French (in)abilities?

THE ORDERLY

B *elgium, May, month thirty-seven*
Gracie screams at everything from a spider to dropping a pencil, so when Gracie was screaming uncontrollably about her ankle Friday night, it was hard to rate the level of seriousness. We were getting ready for Family Movie Night (formerly known as Naked Movie Night, but then we had kids soooo...) and Gracie was in the kitchen on a stool washing her hands when she slipped and rolled her ankle. It swelled a little, but I thought maybe she had been overreacting. Normally she screams out of fear of the worst-case scenario rather than the actual pain or problem. I put ice on it and we watched the movie. Afterward she said she still couldn't walk and so we carried her to bed hoping that a night of sleep would make her forget the ankle. When she woke up Saturday morning and tried to put weight on it, she collapsed and so we decided to head to the ER. Aaron and I played rock, paper, scissors to see who was going to take her and ultimately just decided that because I'm her *doudou* (lovey, blankie, teddy, whatever you call it in your household—in French the *doudou* is a child's comfort) I should go with her. After three years here, I felt my level of French is enough to allow me to comfortably handle the ER. (However, I still begin every single conversation with, "Excuse my French. My level of French is beginner" to allow me some wiggle room.)

We got to the hospital and parked in the ER parking lot and I proceeded to heave Gracie up on my hip to carry her in. This is one instance where I wish I hadn't gotten rid of our strollers. Gracie is your average size five-year-old, but one solid piece of mass. She is literally dead-weight and it confuses everyone who tries to lift her or hold her. A solid fifty pounds that through some magical illusion feels like 100 pounds. Gracie and Ayla weigh the exact same, but it's like night-and-day difference in how it feels. It's like Thor's hammer. It looks so light when he holds it, but no one else can even lift it.

I walked completely lopsided and was panting when we reached the automatic ER doors and they wouldn't open. There was a sign on the doors that I didn't understand and everything looked dark inside. I needed to make a decision quickly or I would have dropped her, so I decided to hop-skip-limp to the front entrance about a hundred yards away. When we got inside, there were security guards there asking if we had an appointment. Breathing heavily, I explained in French that the ER doors are closed and I need to take her in for her foot. One guard looked at the other one realizing that the directions she could give me might not be understood, and that's when I noticed the young man standing off to the side in a white hospital coat with a badge front and center. He looked to be twenty or twenty-one, but his acne-covered face indicated that he might have been a bit younger. He was wearing bottle-cap glasses that were presumably meant to help his eyes, which were both pointed in opposite directions. He was rocking from his heels to his toes and using every ounce of willpower to stay put. He could hardly contain his enthusiasm and finally announced in a forced, deep voice, "Me. I will be the one to take her. It's not a problem. Miss, you can follow me." Within seconds I realized he must have been a volunteer or an orderly intern. He was so excited to have a purpose and show off his hospital navigation skills. He turned to us while walking briskly and pointed to his badge, "I will take you through the hospital in the elevators meant only for personnel. You can't get on these elevators without one of these."

Smiling to myself, I purposefully stroked his ego and said, "We are so lucky to have found you. Thank you for helping us."

"Yes, you are!" he said and turned back around, but not before I saw the corners of his mouth turn up.

About a mile into our Personnel Elevator Tour, he stopped abruptly in the middle of a deserted hallway and quickly glanced around. Not seeing anyone, he turned to us and in a quiet, serious tone, he asked Gracie what happened. It was his moment to shine and assess the problem while no one was around to tell him that he was an intern and not meant to play doctor. When she told him she fell and hurt her ankle, he GRABBED. HER. ANKLE before I could even stop him! She screamed and cried out in pain and he nodded as if that was what he was expecting and wagged his pointer finger in the air saying, "Yep. She needs to go to the Emergency Room." *Um, you think?!* But how could I get mad at him?

When we finally arrived, he proudly used his badge to get us in the back doors of the ER and showed me where the check-in was. This is where it gets really awkward and I'm still laughing out loud just writing this.

I set Gracie down, telling her to stand on one leg and hang on to me while I got out her ID card. I could tell immediately that Mr. Orderly wanted to be as helpful as he could, so he leaned down and attempted to pick Gracie up like a princess. He immediately grunted and groaned, not even able to get her leg off the ground. "Woah," he mumbled while adjusting positions and bending down further.

> Meanwhile, Gracie was gasping every time he tried to lift her and clung to my pant leg. "She's OK, sir. She can just stay there," I said.

"No, no, it's not a problem! I do this all the time." He tried several different positions to lift her and finally turned her around, face out, and heeeeeaved her up under her arms. Trying so hard not to laugh, I reassured Gracie, in English, that I'd be done soon. It was like looking at a little kid trying to carry a cat its same size. Her eyes wide with uncertainty, her arms were straight out, her neck had disappeared, her belly was fully exposed, and her legs were dangling mid-air.

"Mom. Mom. Mom?" she repeated while I was answering questions to the clerk. I looked over again and as if on cue, Mr. Orderly started rocking her back and forth. I turned back to answer a question and immediately heard, "Shhh, shhhh, shhh" coming from Mr. Orderly. Thinking he was shushing me, I turned back to look at him and saw I was mistaken. He wasn't shushing me, he was literally whispering, "Shhh, shhhh, shhh" in Gracie's ear while dangling and rocking her like a newborn baby. A little laugh escaped my mouth that time. Gracie was bug-eyed and starting to slip from his "cat-like hold." Through gritted teeth she begged, "Mommmmmm!!" I smiled and said to Mr. Orderly, "You're so nice, but you don't need to hold her. You can set her in that chair."

"Well," he breathlessly whispered, while still trying to maintain a deep, manly voice, "That's a good idea."

After I finished checking in, I walked over to Gracie and Mr. Orderly and thanked him again for all his help. Wiping little beads of sweat from his forehead, he bowed and said, "My pleasure. I leave you now." He straightened up, spun on his heels, and was out the door. Mr. Orderly left my life just as quickly as he had come into it.

And Gracie's ankle was broken.

THE STEREOTYPE

Belgium, May, month thirty-seven

I just received the funniest call from Analise, Renée's mom. Renée is in Gracie's preschool class and her mom is one of the first women that spoke to me when I got here. She's one of those people that is "in the know." She has "a person" for everything you might need. When I got here, she's the one that saw a flyer for a French class at the convent and sent me the information and then called several times to see if I was attending.

Analise speaks a hundred miles per hour and jumps from topic to topic and I love her so much. The other day we were talking at after school pick-up and I told her about Gracie's birthday party coming up and that I had rented a bounce house. She immediately whipped out her phone and said, "I know a guy. Sixty-five euros the whole day." I told her that we had already rented one, but thank you.

"Yes, but how much?"

"A hundred euros, but it's massive."

"Did you already pay deposit? Cancel. This guy is good." She dropped her voice low as if she had this inside man and it was secret information.

Before I could even make excuses she was on to the next topic. "Alicia," she said, "I went to a farmer's market this morning and honestly, they are the best. You want the address? Here, I'm texting it to you right now. They have the best strawberries. Here, come try one."

I usually just nod and smile and say, "Wow!" and "*C'est vrai*?!" while she's talking because by the time I've formulated a sentence in my head and conjugated everything, she's on to something else. I followed her to the car and she showed me the five boxes of strawberries.

"Here, try one. They're delicious, no? Call your kids over. Kids! You want a box? Here, have a box." I politely declined and told her I'd just go buy one.

"Oh, and they have milk! Fresh cow's milk! Here, take a bottle. Make crepes and send me a picture." She wouldn't take no for an answer, so I finally took the bottle and we left. Later, I got a text from her asking for a photo of the crepes.

So, I was getting ready to walk into the doctor's office when my phone rang and I saw her calling. When I answered she sounded upbeat, but very hurried and serious, which is not unusual. She said, "Alicia. I have a very important question to ask you, so I'm going to speak slowly so you understand everything. I work with a woman who has a brother in Ukraine. He used to be Ukrainian military and he's very sick. He needs to get the help he needs. Do you understand?!"

"Yes, but..." I said before being cut off.

"Alicia. He is so sick. Who do I call?"

Silence. *Um, what?* I literally was struggling to figure out 1) why she called me and 2) was something lost in translation?

"Alicia? Are you there? Who do I call?"

"Um, yes, yes, I'm here. I just...I just don't know, Analise."

"There are some American military members you know, no?"

"Yes, but that doesn't...we wouldn't...we, we..." I trailed off because I was literally so confused. Why was she asking me this? I came up with some vague answer about Aaron not even being in the military. She was so nice and understanding and we got off the phone. I sat there so confused, still am, but then I remembered, this is definitely not the first time this has happened. In all of our years overseas, we've had so many requests for random things and I have a few theories, but the main one is that we're American. Well, it's the main theory because so many of the odd requests include, "But you're American!" Either foreigners have a distaste for Americans or they have completely misconceived notions about us. Granted, there is a range of American types, but I like to think I am pretty much your typical American. We are viewed as either being wealthy beyond measure, able to handle any problem, or culturally isolated. I blame the *Real Housewives* franchise.

When we were in Turkey, we had so many requests for help to get visas to the States. We've had more people than we can count ask for money—which we had heard about and expected, but asking for contact information to help a sick Ukrainian veteran is a new one.

A couple years ago, a woman named Maelys befriended me and asked me to come over to her house one day so she could practice English. We had spent about ten minutes practicing English when she went ahead and launched into her real reason for asking me over. All of a sudden, she became very distraught while telling me how they didn't have much money, but her car needed a new transmission. She said she had heard about this American website called "Go Fund Me." *Oh dear,* I thought as I started to see where this was going. "I heard you can just create an account and people will just give you money from America," she genuinely stated.

I explained to her that, yes, the site existed, but most of the accounts aren't ever funded. When I could see that she thought I just didn't want to help her, I backtracked a little and told her that we weren't allowed to do crowdfunding while working overseas. She said she understood and perked right back up, asking if I could help get her a new iPhone from the States that she heard was so much cheaper without European sales tax.

I had to laugh to myself while trying to follow her thought process. I loved and still love her dearly. We are good friends and she is one of the most honest and real women I know. I can only imagine what preconceived notions others have as well. We all do. I'm convinced that the only way to verify the validity of those notions is to live abroad—and even then we still only see and experience such a small part of a bigger picture.

THE MAMMOGRAM

B*elgium, May, month thirty-seven*
Here's the real question: Can you really say you've lived in another country if you haven't had a breast exam there? Apparently I'm going for the full immersion experience here. A few weeks ago my chest was hurting and felt different. We are just getting ready to move and I didn't want to have to worry about it, so I called the clinic and asked to be seen. Because of the sensitivity—*pun intended*—of the situation, the scheduler said she wanted to get me in right away, but my usual English doctor was unavailable and the only other English-speaking doctor available was the Italian doctor.

"Is it a female?" I asked, trying desperately to push away all the stereotypes of male Italians.

"No, it's a male, but this is his specialty. He's a breast surgeon. He will be the best for this situation." *I'm sure it is his specialty.* Dang those judgmental thoughts. I told her that it was OK and I'd take the appointment.

On my way to the appointment, I debated warning my five-year-old about the nature of the appointment. She happened to be in tow because she broke her ankle, was in a cast, and couldn't make it up the stairs to her classroom in her 150-year-old school.

We've always been open with our kids about the body—especially while living in Europe—and want to normalize it. I've never wanted my girls to be ashamed or embarrassed in their own skin. So I decided that if I brought it up and warned her, then it would become a "thing," so I didn't say anything, hoping she wouldn't notice or think twice about it.

When I was called back by the nurse, a part of me was really not that surprised that with my luck, the nurse was also...an Italian male. Leaving Gracie in the waiting area and following the nurse, I immediately reverted to my coping mechanism for when I'm in uncomfortable situations. I just pretended like I didn't care and was the one in charge, probably sharing more information than I needed to. This is all the same concept as laughing first. If I laugh first, it's OK. If I make them uncomfortable first, then I won't be.

After getting more information than he needed, he told me to follow him and that my daughter should probably come since the exam room was down the hallway. Gracie was oblivious to anything happening since her face was glued to a screen watching something. Once in the exam room, I put Gracie in a corner chair (*"Nobody puts Baby in a corner"...unless your mom is getting a breast exam by a strange man*) and turned around just as the doctor was coming in. He didn't even say hello, but patted the table and told me to strip down waist up and lie down. I stood there awkwardly for a second waiting for a gown or for them to exit the room or at least TURN AROUND, but nooooo, I didn't get the memo. The memo that said they do things differently in Europe.

"Oh. You mean now?"

"Yes. Now. Waist up."

I looked from nurse to doctor and back again. They didn't ever turn around—just waited for me to hurry up. I started scanning the room for a gown or paper or something, anything, and seeing none I just went for it. It only becomes uncomfortable if you let it, right? WRONG.

As I turned around to set my shirt and bra on a chair, Gracie was looking at me—her topless mother—with her eyes bulging out of her head and said, "Uhhh, Mom? This is weeh-ud. Willy weeh-ud." Again not wanting to give her a complex or instill fear regarding the doctors, I just casually said, "Oh not at all, honey—it's not every day you get to be topless in front of two Italian men." Oh my gosh, I'm kidding! I did NOT say that. I said, "Oh not at all, honey. They're doctors and it's always OK if a parent is with you. Plus, it's just a body, remember?" Apparently that satisfied her because she just shrugged and went back to her show and never mentioned it again.

I was secretly *dying* inside, but hopefully, I played it off well. When he was done, he flipped the lights back on—blaring, white, doctor's office lights that are meant to expose every detail—and told me to get dressed while they continued to talk to me like I wasn't some topless woman standing there uncomfortably with my five-year-old in the corner.

Everything looked good, and I left. Later when I told my siblings this whole story, my sister Makay said, "Well—you can check that off your bucket list!"

A few days went by and I got a call from the clinic telling me that the doctor decided he wanted me to go to the local hospital for a mammogram just to be sure and all my records had already been sent over. When I showed up for my mammogram, I was so relieved to see the office was full of women. After my experience at the clinic, I felt prepared for anything. A nurse called me back and took me to a closet. Literally—a closet. It was a room that couldn't have been bigger than 4 feet x 4 feet with nothing but a mirror and hooks on the walls. I turned around immediately and the nurse just told me to undress from the waist up and hang everything on the hooks.

I felt relieved and thought, *Well this is certainly a lot more private than the other clinic!* I undressed and waited for the doctor. As I was standing there with my arms across my chest, the door swung open and I saw the nurse again. She told me to follow her and started walking away. I looked around again for some hidden gown that I was supposed to have put on but didn't see anything. I stuck my head out of the closet-like room and yell-whispered:

"I you follow? Like this? No coat?"

"Yes, of course. Just down the hallway."

Laughing nervously, but trying to play it off as cool, I slowly followed her down. the. hallway. TOPLESS. Past all the other closet rooms. I said, "It is very different from the United States. We have always coat." Either she was confused at my French or she was confused as to why we would do it that way, but she didn't say anything.

We entered a room where the mammogram machine was and after she finished, she took me down another hallway—topless. I was starting to feel like the Emperor in *The Emperor's New Clothes*—except I was the only one that noticed my nakedness and no one else did. She dropped me off with the radiologist, who performed a sonogram. The radiologist explained that everything looked good and there were no problems; I just had fatty breasts. *News to me. I thought all breasts were fatty.*

Finally feeling relieved and grateful, I proudly walked back down the hallway, to my closet. I can now say that I've REALLY lived in another country.

THE DEPARTURE—BELGIUM

B elgium, June, month thirty-eight

FRENCH HAS KEPT ME humble until the very end. It's been a long three years, but I'm not done trying to win you over, French! During all of our goodbyes, and in between my ugly cries, I would tell people, "I'm going to miss you so much!" The only problem was that I was using direct translation in my head. When I say, "I'm going to miss you so much," I translate it to *Je vais te manquer beaucoup,* when in fact that translation says, "You are going to miss me so much!" And I bet they will! Me and my Frenchemy.

Almost exactly three years ago, after I dropped my kids off at their new school, I sat in my car and sobbed like a baby. I wondered if we had made a mistake moving our kids to a new country, new school, and new language. Today, I picked up my kids for the last time at their Belgian school and sat in my car again sobbing, but this time because I was so overwhelmed with emotion as I watched all the friends and teachers surrounding my kids, hugging and crying, saying their goodbyes. It was such a beautiful experience. It was hard, but it was beautiful and it was priceless.

Sunday was also our last day at church and my last day teaching primary. I had a lump in my throat the whole time because each one of these people has a piece of my heart that I know I will leave behind with them. I was already fighting back tears when someone came to pull me in another room for "a picture together." I walked in and saw that the entire congregation had brought food for a goodbye potluck. They had a leather-bound book with letters and notes and pictures to commemorate our time there. After we finished eating, they all stood and sang "God Be With You Till We Meet Again" and I sobbed like a baby who's had their dolly taken away. It wasn't feminine or composed at all. We never would have gotten this experience had we lived near the English-speaking expat community like originally planned. THIS is real wealth—to love and be loved by people who you can't fully communicate with, but with whom you share a true connection.

We will never be monetarily rich in our line of work. We will not be the parents who are able to give their kids whatever they want, but what we can give them are memories and experiences. While living here and not paying a mortgage, we saved money each month with the idea in mind that we would build or move into a bigger home back in the States. As our departure neared, we asked the kids if they would rather have a newer, nicer home with all the money we saved while living here or if they would rather stay in our smaller, older home but have money to travel and return to Belgium to visit their friends and practice their French. All three of them unanimously opted for a small home with travel options. That has to say something, right?

THE MEANTIME—PART II

U SA—*First six months back*
Once again I find myself in the bittersweet transition phase
of having left something I've grown to absolutely love and returning to
what was once so hard for me to leave. Before leaving Belgium, I had
that same pit in my stomach as I did when preparing to leave Turkey. I
knew a phase in my life was ending and a new one was beginning. The
apprehension of transition is what gets me. The apprehension of the
unknown. I wish I could just skip the transition period and fast
forward six months where I'm already settled into the new phase of life.

Before leaving, I started making a list of all the things I was excited
for in the US to help make leaving Belgium easier for me.

- Costco's Kirkland toilet paper. Don't laugh. You go
overseas and try living without great, inexpensive toilet
paper.

- Mexican food. You don't know what you're missing until
your country is no longer sharing a massive border with
Mexico.

- Being able to wear gym clothes or yoga pants in public
without being stared down. I might as well have worn curlers
in my hair and a bathrobe because I got the same look either
way.

- Calories posted next to menu items. This would have come in really useful next to all the *frites*, *eclairs*, and *pain au chocolat*. I kept thinking the *pain au chocolat* tasted so light and airy that there was no way it could be unhealthy to eat every day.

- Cheaper dish detergent. Holy moly. I had to sell my hair just to afford the dish detergent. I *almost* just resorted to washing dishes the old-fashioned way.

- Window screens. OK, now, for a continent that doesn't believe in air-conditioning and likes to sleep with windows open, WHERE ARE THE WINDOW SCREENS. We tried to leave them open a few times, but after the third bat in the house, we gave up. I'll never forget my husband swinging around a broom in the hallway and ducking for cover.

- Free public toilets. It's really inconvenient to try and find change in your pockets when you have to "go," especially when you don't have any so you head to an ATM and the smallest bill is twenty euros, so you walk to the coffee shop to get smaller bills and finally make your way to the public toilets with your pants already soiled.

- Public toilets. They're few and far between. It makes perfect sense why people just pee on the side of the road.

- Free water

- Free refills on drinks

- Not having uncomfortable, embarrassing situations.

This list helps, but I'm already planning our next overseas adventure and still have one foot out the door. We're addicted and love it. I'm not sure when we will go, but for the foreseeable future, we need to be here for our kids.

Our kids still speak *Frenglish* at home. They have a French tutor, a French babysitter and only watch shows in French. I'm not about to let three years of blood, sweat and tears go to waste. We didn't learn a new language just to forget it. We used to think the *Frenglish* was funny, but now that we're back, we're working hard to undo some habits. For example, Ayla always asks, "What day are we?" just like they do in French. I can't get her to say, "What day is it?" for the life of me. The girls can't get out of the habit of saying, "I will explain you..." or "Will you explain me?" when trying to explain something *to* someone.

When we arrived in the US, it took all of a few days for us to quickly realize we needed to "re-Americanize" our kids. While visiting my parents, we took the kids to visit a cave. At the end of the tour, they had us sit in an amphitheater of sorts and played a patriotic movie projected onto a wall of stalactites with Celine Dion singing the National Anthem. Some of the elderly in the room were tearing up and it was very moving until Gracie leaned over to me and loudly whispered, "Uhh this is widiculous!" Apparently she wasn't moved. I laughed and when the show ended I headed over to Aaron to tell him what Gracie had said. However, before I could even say anything, he said, "Ayla just leaned over to me and told me that was 'ridiculous.'" I started laughing that two out of three of our children had said the same thing. Then our son walked up to us and said, "Well, that was weird!" OK, three out of three of our kids. Soooo, we immediately bought fireworks and matching red, white, and blue outfits for the Fourth of July. They were in heaven. I think we converted Gracie, but Ayla, ever skeptical and more of a French/Belgian patriot, is not so easily swayed. She tells people she is half Turkish and half French-Belgian, which has surprised a few people when they meet me or Aaron and we clearly are neither.

We are now accustomed to explaining that our kids are more of Third Culture Kids, a term coined by Ruth Hill in the 1950s and widely known in the expat community. Third Culture kids spend a majority of their formative years in a country or culture that differs from that of their parents. They don't fully identify with their native country's culture, nor the foreign country's culture. They're somewhere in between—thus the term Third Culture. While some might instinctively pity Third Culture Kids, for being seemingly "stuck" or "lost," I believe they possess a quality that so many of their peers lack. They possess a sense of cultural awareness that no amount of travel can instill. The world is not just something they hear and read about, or visit for a few days; the world is something they experience up close and personal. I can tell they view things in a different light. They're interested in learning about other countries and world news and they're more aware and accepting of other cultures than they were before living overseas.

While I miss the adventure of living in new places, I'm fully embracing the familiarity and comfort of living stateside. I love that I can pick up the phone and call the plumber and not fumble my way through scheduling repairs while unknowingly insulting him in the process. I love being able to just stop by a friend's house or call a neighbor to borrow a cup of milk if needed. I was missing this sense of community that I lacked due to living in the countryside and being foreign. The minute we returned home, we had offers to stay at people's homes until our household goods arrived, and meals were dropped off for us. People showed up to help us unpack and clean.

One of the women that came to help me clean is my secret best friend. I say "secret" because she just doesn't know it yet. She's about twenty-five years older than me and I idolize her. She's like a younger, warmer, American version of the Queen of England. She's classy sophisticated, and soft-spoken. I see her as a friend of the same age, but I think because she has a daughter my age, she may not feel the same way. Because I follow her cycling excursions on Instagram, I started talking to her about wanting to be her new biking partner. Basically, I am forcing myself into her life.

"Rachel! Next time you go cycling, I want to go too! We would have so much fun!" She graciously obliged and we set a date. Now, there are a few things to know about this situation that I grossly underestimated. I knew she had a proper cycling bike, but I thought that being twenty-five years younger than her would make up for not having the proper equipment. You know, my youthful stamina against her few-thousand-dollar road bike. You guys. As if the universe hasn't humbled me enough, it decided to throw in the grand finale.

Thinking I had a few weeks to unpack and oil my bike, I put it off until Rachel texted one day and explained that she had an event on the date we originally had planned and asked if we could go the following morning instead.

Trying to act cool and nonchalant, I responded, "Hi! Yes, that would be great. What time do you want to go? I need to put air in my tires and oil on my brakes." I was completely unprepared—but you do NOT say no to the queen. (I was totally fan-girling her).

I heard another text come in from Rachel that read, "Would leaving as soon as your children are at school work for you? Do you have a pump and the oil you need? [*No, but I could just use olive oil, right?*] Also, do you know how far you would like to go? [*I could totally do seven to eight miles, but maybe she's not up for that. I should say five to six to sound less presumptuous.*] Often we meet at my house and bike into the city...[*Wait. What? The CITY? Girl, no*]....to any of the museums and explore them a bit. Sometimes we metro home and this ends up being 18 to 21 miles. [*What. is. Happening?!?!*] Or sometimes we have biked home as well and this is usually 34 to 37 miles." [*Demon, be gone! No she didn't! She's some kind of cyclist ninja demon.*]

"I'm seriously up for whatever. The city sounds great," I said. *Liar.*

So I did what any commoner would do when they're about to have tea, or a bike ride from hell, with the queen. I group-texted my sisters a screenshot of Rachel's text to me and watched their responses roll in...

Sister 3: "AAAAAHHHHHH. NO. hahahahahaha. The answer is no, Alicia."

Sister 1: "Hahahaha. Do it Alicia. You have to."

Sister 2: "Hahahaha. Do it!"

Sister 1: "Oil? Whyyyy do you need oil?" *Clearly, we are not cyclists in our family.*

Sister 2: "How cool is she?! Wait, does she think you're an actual biker? Hahahaha. Like does she have a whole outfit? I guarantee her bike is at least 2k."

Me: "Mmmmk. I'm so nervous to go with her now."

Sister 1: "Ask her if she has an extra bike handy that you could borrow."

Not pleased with the moral support I was getting, I ignored the fact that there would be a "next day" and that I needed to get my bike out. That evening after the kids were in bed, I finally let the panic sink in and ran out to the shed where my bike was—exceppppt unbeknownst to me, my bike was still in a couple pieces from the move. I dragged it through the yard and back to the carport, where I attempted to put it back together in the dark. When I say "it," I mean the $99 bike I bought at Walmart thirteen years ago simply as a commuter bike to the metro in the mornings. I know, I know, what in the actual heck was I thinking trying to go biking on a mule against a stallion?

Finally pleased with my bike assembly skills, I jumped on it to make sure it wouldn't fall apart and immediately realized there was no place to put my feet. The pedals were on backward, as well as the handlebars. *Glad I noticed that now!* Forty-five minutes later, and way past my bedtime, I wiped all the dirt and cobwebs off (literally) and patted the seat, crossing my fingers that it would work. I headed upstairs and crawled into bed.

The next morning, I threw on some workout clothes and got my kids ready for school. I put the seats down in the van to transport my bike and let me tell you, one doesn't normally take a good look at the state of their bike until they're about to go cross-country with a semi-professional. What a sad, sad, little, bike.

I was already running late to drop my kids off at school when I realized that I didn't have a helmet. I quickly rummaged through the sports bin until I found one that I thought would work and threw it in the back of the van. I arrived at Rachel's a few minutes late and a bit frazzled. I hurried to get my bike out of the van and ride it down the sidewalk to her house. I jumped on the bike with my helmet in hand and started pedaling—only I didn't go anywhere. I spun and spun my feet until the bike—and I—tipped over. The bike chain had come off. *Crap.*

"Rachel, I'm here. Just adjusting my bike chain," I texted her. A few minutes later her garage door started opening and I could see her legs standing in the garage. Then everything happened in slow motion. As the door was rising, there stood a woman in a fancy cyclist outfit with cycling shoes, wisps of hair blowing in the wind under her shiny helmet. In slow motion, I looked from my old running shoes, up to my yoga pants and ratty tank top, and back again at Rachel. Queen Rachel. My one-sided best friend. Time sped up again and she walked over just as I was putting the chain back on the spokes. *Are they even called spokes? I have no idea what that little circular pointy thing that holds the chain is called.* I jumped up and cheerfully greeted her. She went back to the garage to retrieve her bike and as she was coming back out, the slow-motion started again. That sleek, red, expensive road bike with thin wheels, perfect for going twenty or more miles. Trying not to show my embarrassment, I fumbled with my helmet, trying to get it on. She stood there patiently while I checked the straps to make sure they weren't tangled and pretended to adjust them, not really knowing why the helmet wouldn't go on. Finally, I just rested it on top of my head and pulled the straps over my cheekbones as hard as I could to get them to clasp around my chin.

We were off! I followed her to the end of the block where we would cross the street to the bike path and as soon as she slowed down, I followed suit and squeezed on my brakes. The screeching sound that ensued made everyone in a block radius grimace and jump. Rachel turned around to me and kindly smiled, asking sweetly if I had a chance to oil the brakes yet. I told her I did, but maybe not enough. What I didn't tell her was that I may or may not have used some PAM cooking spray all over the bike because I couldn't really find where to oil the brakes. So we continued. About a mile into the ride, I realized that I was having to squeeze harder and harder on the brakes to get it to slow and I mentally calculated that I would need to start squeezing the brakes about twenty feet ahead of the stopping point to be able to fully come to a stop. I kept that to myself. After about twenty or thirty minutes I was dying. I figured that at the pace we were going we should have been halfway there. We chatted about our families and I asked her anything to distract myself from the pain. At one point Rachel said "This next part is the hardest part of the ride because it's straight uphill for a while. It gets narrow, so I will just ride ahead of you and we can stop at the top." LIAR. She did NOT tell me it was a hill from hell. She did not tell me that my heart would pound so hard I could feel it in my eyelashes. She did not tell me that I would start seeing stars. I still don't know how I made it up that hill. On the way we passed some construction workers and I could see them all watching this very light-haired woman easily cruising up this hill and then turn to see me lagging a hundred feet behind her and using every. single. part. of my body to ride up that hill. Shame. That's what that feeling is called.

At the top of the hill, Rachel was waiting for me. I was genuinely worried we were going to have to call an ambulance. I thought for sure

I would pass out. When I stepped off the bike, my legs gave out and I fell down, but I immediately pretended that I dropped down to check on my chains and wheels. *Please, dear universe, let me not faint.* Rachel finished her water and checked her watch, announcing that we had made it five miles. *FIVE MILES*, people. What in the name of the Tour de France was she saying? Five meant that we had at least thirteen more to go.

The next few miles were uneventful, *hallelujah*, and I ignored the throbbing pain that had started between my legs and the seat. Every now and then we needed to form a single file line while we passed someone. At one point, I got behind Rachel while someone was passing on the other side when immediately she had to slam on her brakes because another biker pulled in front of her. With adrenaline rushing, I squeezed my brakes as hard as I could...but didn't slow at all. Something happened and my brakes had just stopped working altogether. *Traitors.* In a split second, I swerved to the left of Rachel so as not to rear-end her and immediately saw a rollerblader in the lane. I swerved back to the center hoping to miss the rollerblader on my left and Rachel and the other cyclist on my right. Up ahead my bike finally slowed and when Rachel caught up to me I said, "Sorry! I wasn't expecting to brake so quickly and I think there's a little (*huge*) problem with my brakes." *Like, they're not working, at all, kind of problem.*

After a while, the pain from my "seat area" was so intense that letting someone hit me with a hammer there would have felt better. Just before the city, we came to the river and I told Rachel I needed a drink of water. *Lie.* So we stopped. Mistake #43 on this little adventure. We should have kept going because the pain getting off the seat was akin to an arrow going through your body—which obviously would be painful—but then having to pull it out. I almost vomited when I got off. I stood there for a second until the stars disappeared from my vision and started to prop up my bike. When I kicked the kickstand with my foot, it fell off. The kickstand. literally. fell. off. You cannot make this stuff up. Extremely embarrassed about my state of being and that of my bike, if you can even call it a bike at that point, I explained that it had been in storage and "was taken apart in our move and I've been meaning to buy a new one, but with all the move expenses, I just haven't gotten around to it yet." Ever gracious and classy, Rachel did not for one second make me feel awkward. After sitting and snacking for a while, I nonchalantly asked how much further it was to the metro. She said we had about three or four more miles left and it was a good thing I was wearing sunglasses because my eyes filled with tears.

"Did you want to take the metro then? We can metro back or bike back."

Rachel, I would literally die right here on the path if I rode back another eighteen miles.

"We should probably metro back so I'm home in time to get the kids from school. Is that OK? By the way, how are you feeling? Because my crotch is a little sore, but other than that, this is great!" *This day is just one big lying game.*

"I'm great! Are you not wearing padded shorts? I have padded cyclist shorts so I don't feel anything," she said. Padded shorts. Of course she did. Whyyyyy on God's green Earth did I not grab my husband's to wear? I didn't even think about that.

"No, I'm not, un-for-tu-nate-ly. They're still in a box somewhere and I'm not sure where they are." *Probably with my non-existent cycling outfit, shoes, and properly fitting helmet.*

I painfully tried to adjust back on my bike seat. I might as well have taken the seat completely off because, at that point, there was no difference in the feeling. I don't know how I made it to the metro. Truly. It's by the grace of God that I got there and bought a ticket and got on the train.

Feeling a little peppier since I was now seated on a proper seat and about to ride home for the next thirty minutes, we continued th in-depth conversation we had been having. Five minutes into the ride, something started to feel off. First, I noticed I was sweating profusely. Then Rachel stopped talking and told me I looked really pale. *For the love of all humanity, please, please, don't get sick on this train. Please let me save a little bit of my dignity in front of this classy friend who hasn't so much as sweat a drop the entire day.*

I knew that feeling. Motion sickness. I used to get it all the time when I was pregnant and commuting into the city for work on the metro. I once vomited into a trash can as soon as I got off. Only I wasn't pregnant this time—just a wannabe cyclist who pushed herself too far. I tried to play it off and just told her I was going to put my head between my knees because this "happens all the time." We continued to talk while I sat there upside down and after about fifteen minutes I started to feel a little better. I sat up and immediately the wave of nausea flooded over me and bile rose in my throat. I threw my head back down between my legs, practically touching the floor, and prayed my little heart out. Rachel was so sweet and kept talking and telling me stories. I didn't hear any of them.

We made it to our stop and I stumbled out the door, forcing one foot in front of the other. It was then I realized that we had to BIKE back to her house. Sick and aching, I willed myself to make it the last mile. TWENTY-ONE miles total. As soon as we got back to her house, I said goodbye and got in the car as fast as I could and drove out of sight—about a block—and pulled over and prepared to vomit in a grocery sack in my car. I never did, but I sat there for ten minutes until the feeling subsided.

Immediate text messages with my sisters:

Me: I have NEVER experienced this kind of pain before.

Sister 1: Are you home?! Take an ice bath!

Me: Truly. I'm in so much pain. Haha. 21 miles. I think my biggest problem was that I was practically riding a tricycle. I need a new bike.

(I sent a photo of me and Rachel)

Sister 1: I love this so much!

Sister 2: You did it!!! I feel like you should get into this.

Sister 2: Wait, Alicia, is your helmet just foam?

What? I zoomed in and enlarged the photo. It *was* just foam! Where was the hard, plastic cover?! I grabbed my helmet and saw little remnants of hard plastic proving that there once was a hard covering over the foam.

Me: Hahahaha. Um, yes. The top must have fallen off.

Sister   2:
Hahahahahahahahahahahahahahahahahahahahahahahaha

Sister 1: Hahahahahahaha I am dying!! This just gets better and better.

I took about 600mg of Ibuprofen and walked like I was sitting on a saddle for the rest of the day. The next day when I woke up, everything from my hair follicles to my toenails hurt. What had I been thinking? Why on earth did I not just confess that I was in no shape to ride twenty-one miles? Ibuprofen became my best friend – it took the spot of Rachel who was just unknowingly bumped to Second Best friend. That evening, I attended the dinner event that Rachel was helping to host.

"Rachel! How are you feeling after yesterday??"

"You know, I've never felt so good after a ride into the city. I feel great!"

Of course. Of course you do.

"How do you feel, Alicia?"

"You know, I feel like someone took a hammer to my nether regions, but pretty good. Pretty good."

The ladies sitting at the table wanted to know what we had done and so when Rachel went to check on the food, I proceeded to tell them what a rockstar she is and how I literally ate her dust the entire way. I told them the whole story about the chain and the kickstand and the brakes. We were all laughing so hard that tears were running down our faces. Other tables started to turn and look at us. Rachel walked back over and I told her that I was recounting how she schooled me in cycling.

"Rachel, *why* didn't you tell me that my helmet was just foam?!" The entire table erupted in laughter when they heard that and I pulled out my phone to show them the picture.

"I didn't even notice! Let me see the picture." When I showed her the picture of us in our helmets, Rachel started laughing even harder. Wiping her classy tears from her classy eyes, she said, "Alicia, WHY is your helmet on backward?!"

I couldn't breathe after that.

Welcome back to the United States, Alicia! This whole time I thought the awkward situations I found myself in were directly related to foreign cultural experiences and language barriers. It turns out, it's just me.

At least I'm laughing first.

THE END

Printed in Great Britain
by Amazon

12382822R00137